Lost In The System

A Foster Parent's Diary

B. J. Davis

Lost In The System

A Foster Parent's Diary

B. J. Davis

Copyright © 1998
All Rights Reserved

ISBN 1-55630-511-7

PUBLISHED BY:
BRENTWOOD CHRISTIAN PRESS
4000 BEALLWOOD AVENUE
COLUMBUS, GEORGIA 31904

DEDICATED TO FOSTER PARENTS PAST, PRESENT, AND FUTURE

Dear Lord,

First, I want to thank Almighty You for calling on me for this job to do.

I've never known before of such joys as I've had watching your little girls and boys.

Thanks for the energy that I knew wasn't mine, and the enthusiasm it took all the time.

I'll always be grateful to you for choosing us to be with your little ones through their heartache and fuss.

We tried so hard and sometimes we failed, but you would pick us up and make us feel compelled.

To start over with each child was our hope to give them a better chance at life so they could cope.

We loved each one – big, little, white or black. We loved them as individuals, or in a pack.

They would take our patience to the very end, then do something cute to make us begin again.

Some days they would age us by 10 years, then days they would make us feel 30 years younger than our peers.

Thank you for what each one has added to our life, with their own personality and each carrying their own strife.

The trouble they have been through saddens me, and the outcome, only you can see.

You, we count on through our difficult days, and we thank you for showing us the finest ways.

The memories we treasured are ever so sweet, and the blessings we've received are such a treat.

In Jesus' Name,
B.J. and Sarge

CONTENTS

Allen 8
Ronnie 9
Bubba. 15
Misti. 19
Paul 20
Eddie 24
Matthew. 25
Rae. 26
Mimi 28
Jeremy 31
Loretta 32
Lawrence 33
Ryan. 34
Rhonda. 35
Ron 36
Julie 37
Gene. 41
Mike. 51
Ray. 52

Sunni	52
Cleta	54
Mark	55
Justin	56
Karen	57
Reggie	58
Mikey	60
Kathy	63
Clinton	63
Anne	64
Buddy	66
Luke	66
Lewis	69
Jimmy	70
Bud	72
John	73
Alena	74
Common Sense and Childhood Handicaps	75
Adoption Crisis	88
Personal Satisfaction	89

INTRODUCTION

Foster parenting wasn't my idea, but rather God's and Sarge's (my husband). It worked out great because Sarge did most of the work and I got most of the credit.

Sarge retired from his supervisory position in a local manufacturing plant and I retired at age three and haven't wanted to work since then. We were ready to retire with all the laid back, do nothing fantasies we could come up with. We figured God would go along with our plan for our kids to respect our age and wait on us hand and foot. We were ready to really play our old age and feeble minds for all they were worth.

We had a 76 year old widowed cousin that was a foster parent. She told Sarge's sister about all the good feelings she was experiencing. His sister, in turn, told him that he would be great with kids and Texas needed more foster parents. We had just gotten our last dependent out of the nest. Boy, was I ready to settle down and sleep 15 hours a day and eat the rest of the hours away.

Sarge mentioned how much fun it would be to have little feet around the house again. Well, Sarge and I have a different view of what's fun. I figured our cousin had told all the good stuff and had left out all the rough parts about fostering. Sure enough, I was right.

God was really working on Sarge but thank goodness He was not making me feel led to take on more cooking, cleaning, wiping noses and other places, changing diapers, washing more clothes, drying more clothes, putting away more clothes, pressing more clothes, patching more clothes, washing more dishes, drying more dishes, putting away more dishes, making more beds, listening to yelling, screaming, crying, fighting, mixing formula, and washing bottles. I knew this stuff would be every day. I also knew these did not count the unexpected hazards of everyday living.

I could see where we would be saving face by telling people that foster care was sure cutting down on our social life, especially when we didn't have a social life in the first place. I could use this as an excuse to make me feel like we would really be jet-setters if it weren't for our obligations to our kids.

Sarge suggested we just try it and if didn't work out for us we could go for another kind of adventure. We decided to start out easy and baby sit our ill cousin's little foster child.

ALLEN

Allen was one of five children who had been neglected and abused. He was nine months old when we met him. His ears seemed quite large for his little head but this was over shadowed by his big smile and two shining front teeth. He was so clean and smelled so good that we just took it for granted this would be the way all our babies would be presented to us. Boy, were we wrong!

Allen was such a sweet young boy who loved to laugh. He was treated well and loved much all the months our cousin had him. We baby sat for three weeks, then it was time for him to go back to his birth parents. When we got him all dolled up and took him to the Children's Protective Service (C.P.S.) Office, we realized that the mama and daddy were collecting all five of their kids from foster homes from all over the county. It made us sad to see that the children weren't happy about the reunion. Our Allen didn't know better and showed no emotion either way, but the older children expressed sadness to have to leave their foster parents.

Within two years we saw them in the system again, and all were with different foster parents. The mom and dad just couldn't give up satisfying their own desires and lost their children.

After going to classes for 30 hours – three hours a week for 10 weeks, and getting the approval of the health and fire departments, as well as being C.P.R. certified, we got our license. We were ready to make a difference in America's children. Bring um on, we were ready. We could not wait to use all of our vast knowledge and skills plus what we had learned from Linda, our class instructor. We started out with such eagerness and enthusiasm, although we were encouraged not to become emotionally involved in the children's lives. We let C.P.S. know we just wanted ages one through five. We love the babies. We didn't feel that God was calling us to take in teenagers, or we sure hoped that wasn't His plan. We couldn't take all the smart back-talk, cussing, threats, runaways, and just plain rudeness, drugs, and sexual activities. We have friends that keep 12 teenagers. They are great and strong people that love the older kids. Sarge and I have had 36 little ones and I would like to tell you a little about these little munchkins that stole our hearts.

I changed all of their names so I wouldn't accidentally embarrass them or cause them any heartache if they ever had the opportunity to read about themselves in my book.

RONNIE

The call came from C.P.S. They had two little brothers and it didn't take us long to decide we would love to take them in. We got our glad rags on and hurried up to the office and were determined to make a good impression on our new little family. When we arrived they told us that the youngest boy wouldn't be there until the following day. We would have to wait another day before we could meet Bubba, but Ronnie was more than glad to meet us.

As we looked down at his handsome face, he looked up at Sarge and asked, "Are you my new daddy?" Sarge said, "Yes." Ronnie jumped up into Sarge's arms and said, "Hi Daddy, let's go home." I nearly cried right there. Then it was explained to Ronnie, and us too, that this was just to be an initial meeting so that we could decide if we wanted them. Ronnie wasn't buying their reasoning at all. He grabbed Sarge and yelled, "Lets go Daddy," as if they could make a get away. C.P.S. tried to explain the rules to Ronnie, but he assured them he wasn't playing by their rules. He cried so broken hearted that C.P.S. realized that sometimes they must bend the rules, especially after we assured them that this was the little boy we wanted. So we put Ronnie into our van and went home.

Sarge made their bedroom/playroom into a fantasy land. He made the bunk beds kid tough and dresser drawers to match with teddy bears painted on them. He used plywood to draw and cut out large replicas of Mickey Mouse and Minnie Mouse and hung them on two walls. On the other walls he had big dinosaurs that had knobs to hold caps, hats, and coats. The toy box Sarge built was a large cradle. He built a smaller cradle for the baby dolls that we hoped would please the little girls we would get some day.

As we pulled into the driveway, Ronnie started to giggle and kept giggling as we went into the house. We pointed him in the direction of the playroom. As he looked around, his eyes got so wide and the biggest grin came over his pretty little face and said, "This will work." He didn't come with any clothes but he was clean because he came to us from other foster parents. C.P.S. wanted the brothers to live together. We got them because we were willing to take them both. Ronnie was excited about having his own bed and fell asleep fast that first night. Sarge and I went in to look at him every 10 minutes, just in case he needed us. He was three years old.

The next day we returned to C.P.S. to meet, and bring home Bubba. The previous foster parents had him for six days, so he was shiny clean. It was easy to see why he was called Bubba. He was built like a big tough eighteen wheeler. He had a broad body and a big round, pretty face. He was 16 months old and had a beautiful smile that later let him get by with more than he should have. We now had a good start as foster parents with a three year old and a 16 month old. We were told their mom was in a women's shelter after having been beaten by their daddy.

Ronnie took fast possession of his new family and really felt comfortable with us as his new mama and daddy. All of our kids called us Mama and Daddy because we were just that while they were with us. We never wanted to take the place of the birth parents, but we did become protective of each of our babies when we raised them as if they were our own kids.

My Mama lived alone in her home across town, here in Conroe. I would go check on her three or four times a week, trying to catch her at home so I could feel I was kinda watching after her. She was still able to drive and was very active in church activities and I knew she could contact me if she needed me. One day while making my run to Mama's I had Ronnie with me. He was my ratting around buddy. As we drove through town, he yelled, "Get down, there's a cop." I realized he came from a home that policemen visited frequently, and had been taught no respect for the law. I tried to explain to him that the man in the car was a policeman, and he would protect us. We could count on him when we were in trouble. He got up from the floor board and said, "It sure looked like a cop." Evidently, I wasn't very convincing. Late one evening after we and the kids finished our errands, we stopped by Long John Silver's and picked up a large family box of fish, shrimp, and french fries. We were very tired when we got home so we all took a bite or two from our big box, and voted to save the rest for lunch the next day. The next morning when I opened the refrigerator I noticed the big Long John Silver's box was missing. I went to Ronnie's bedroom and asked if he had seen our lunch. He said, "Who took it?" He jumped from his bottom bunk bed and yelled, "Lets find him." When he jumped, the sheet moved enough that a box from Long John Silver's could be seen under his bed. He just looked up real sheepishly and asked, "Did we find him?" He left very few crumbs, and it's a wonder that he didn't need to be hospitalized and admitted to the Intensive Care Unit. This time, as in a few other instances, he didn't get into much trouble. I could have been more effective if he hadn't heard me laugh when he asked, "Did we find him?"

The advantage of Sarge and me being older foster parents is that we didn't expect the kids to be perfect, as we would have liked our birth children to be. We can be more understanding and can teach them that the most important things in life, aren't things.

We tried to teach them proper manners and respect for authority so life would be easier for them after they left us. They knew how to say yes mam, yes sir, excuse me, thank you, and please. When leaving the dinner table, they learned to say, "May I be excused, please?" These are all such easy words to learn, especially when they find it so easy to mimic every commercial on television. They were taught to apologize when they were wrong so it wouldn't be so hard to do as they got older. It would just come natural for them. They were taught that a clean conscience would make a soft pillow and the result would be a good nights sleep.

Ronnie never mentioned anything about missing his parents and seemed so pleased living with us. He became more aggressive as time went on and our love for him grew more and more. We loved him, not for his aggressiveness, but because we felt he needed us more.

He loved Batman and had to have his daily wear and pajamas with the Batman theme. When he and I would go into the local stores, he was always addressed as Batman. He loved it and played the part to the hilt.

We enrolled him in Head Start, a program designed for young children of poor families, which was definitely us, and he really took charge. The school bus would meet us at our church, Mims Baptist. As we sat up at the church waiting on the bus he asked, "Where does the church live?" The driver always looked so disappointed when she saw our van. She only had him for 45 minutes. The poor teachers had him until 2:00 PM. Every day was something new with Ronnie. The teachers loved him because of his outgoing personality. He loved all of them so much that he even asked one teacher to marry him.

Ronnie was so very strong and very destructive. One day when he came home I asked, "Baby, how was your day?" He said, "Mama, one time today I had them all mad at me." He was used to three or four being mad at him but not everyone at once.

Although the state did not terminated his daddy's parental rights, Ronnie pleaded with us that he should never have to see him again. I told him he was safe now and his Bad Daddy (as he called him) was history. Ronnie's interpretation of my statement was, "That's good, Bad Daddy's hippie." When he would have sad thoughts he would come up to me and give me a big hug and say, "Aren't you glad that Bad Daddy's hippie?"

We tried to really get him into the rodeo spirit and got him a cowboy suit and cowboy boots. Big mistake! We didn't count on him using the kids and teachers as footballs with his new boots. That very day Head Start changed some of their rules about wearing boots to school, and we agreed. Of course, little Ronnie helped change lots of rules for that school.

I remember when my daughter, Julie Anne, and I decided to take Ronnie and Julie Anne's boys, Bubba and Buddy, to the Dollar Movie to see Jurassic Park. Ronnie enjoyed it so much I could tell his mind was right in the park with all the dinosaurs. It was so very quiet at the end of the show. Everyone was in silent thought as the birds slowly flew away into the sky. Then little Ronnie said loud enough to be heard all over the theater, "Good-bye birdies." Everyone seemed to like the way he broke the ice and got us all back to reality.

When Julie Anne and I would have to run to the grocery store in our van she would circle the parking lot with all four kids while I'd dash in to get the milk. When I came out, she pulled the van up and I thought I could get in with them. Just as I got close, Julie Anne thought it would be funny if they would pull out and circle again with me standing there like a fool. Just as they got close to picking me up again Ronnie would say, "Lets leave Mama again." And then all five of them would scream with laughter. Finally, they felt sorry for the old fat lady holding the milk, and after picking me up, laughed all the way home.

Ronnie loves to laugh at himself and at others. He thought he was real funny and we all agreed he had a sense of humor at times, but there were occasions when he had a sense of seriousness as well. He could ask such deep questions that for a shallow person like me, I'd have to call for help to satisfy some of his curiosity.

When he would act up I'd always say, "That behavior is not accepted and won't be tolerated." As time went on I would catch him telling the other kids, especially when he wasn't getting his way, "That haver's not cepted and won't be rated." So I was proud that he was at least hearing some of the things I was trying to teach him.

BUBBA

Now, let me tell you about our Bubba. Try to see him as I did. He was an overwhelming preciousness that had a big smile and a low, loud, laugh that just melted your heart. As I looked at him, never in my mind would I have believed that this pretty, round, full faced darling would ever allow an evil thought in that good looking head of his.

Well, we've all heard the term, "Beauty is skin deep but ugly goes all the way to the bone." His orneriness went all the way through that handsome body. It became apparent to us when he was in the crib that we weren't dealing with a plain vanilla kid. He started out by taking the playpen apart, corner by corner, and hitting the china cabinets to see how fast we could move to protect our dishes that we thought meant so much to us.

Then at night in his baby bed he would shake the bed and let out a Tarzan yell. He was so strong. We could scold him or baby him, pacify him or rock him. He just didn't get it. We were in trouble if we did not keep our eyes on him at all times and even then, trouble was just around the corner. This was not a child that felt the need to sneak around and do his evil deeds. He could perform with or without an audience. He thought he had achieved a good days work if he took the padding out of the baby bed mattress and pulled down some drapes in a bedroom.

C.P.S. gave us a reimbursement of $15.85 a day to help defray the cost of diapers, milk, clothes, and all the other expenses, not counting our labor or time. But when a person goes into this line of work, it is understood that it's not a money making adventure.

Little Bubba would cause more damage to one house and one yard than a demolition crew could have been paid to do. We could talk to him for hours and explain to him in his language, (which I think was Chinese), how this behavior was not acceptable and would not be tolerated. He could flash a big smile and say, "Wets eat, my tummy's ungry."

Bubba could be just as lovable as he was ornery. He would sit in your lap, wanting you to sing to him. The singing part always got to me because my own kids asked me not to sing to them. But Bubba appreciated my squeaking voice that never was on key and seldom produced the right words. When he fell asleep for another night, I could almost forget how many windows, lamps, or glasses he had broken that day.

Around the house, many times I'd call Sarge "Honey." Bubba liked that, and started calling him "Daddy Honey." As Christmas drew nearer, we'd get excited about the holidays. We probably went overboard to get them toys, since it would be special for them.

We were told that an aunt and uncle of the kids were willing to take them in and they would be leaving us. They picked one week before Christmas to make such a big change. in all of our lives. We asked if they couldn't stay at least until the first of the year, but I guess that would make it too easy for everyone, so we made plans for a big Christmas party before they left.

Other foster parents told us that C.P.S. was donating $40.00 for each kid. The amounts varied, depending on the age of the child. We thought this was good news because we had spent gobs more than that. We asked for our money and were told there would be none at all because our children wouldn't be with us on Christmas Day. We assured them that our babies would have a great Christmas with us, and we were pleased to foot the bill alone.

Sarge's sisters, our kids, and two ladies from my Sunday School Class all surprised us with gifts for them. You might think our babies were living with the rich and famous. They had the time of their lives.

We all cried, and tried to explain the rules as best we could to them so they would be happy with their aunt, uncle, and cousins in Florida. About three months later C.P.S. called and said, "Things are just not working out with our boys, so could they come home to you?" We were excited to get them back. The caseworker who flew out there to bring them back says she was afraid the other passengers on the plane were going to throw our boys off before she could get them to us. Those little imps did not want seat belts and didn't want to stay in their assigned seats. They reasoned that any people on the plane would change seats with them, and they thought it only fair to give the people a chance to play musical chairs to kill the monotony. This was probably the only time that plane full of people clapped when two passengers got off.

We had Bubba checked for his behavior and the doctors said it was the worst case of Attention Deficit Disorder they had ever seen. He must have been lacking something in his diet because he started biting any child that got close to him. As the months went by I guess he decided not to make a career as a cannibal and realized other kids gave him a bad taste. You might think Bubba was hard to love, but to know him was to love him. He could be so sweet and loving at times. Other times he would have a Hyde and Jekyll personality.

Ronnie's and Bubba's mama and daddy were still fighting drugs, alcohol, and with each other too.

Their great grandparents started visiting with us. They were such sweet, caring people, who were raising Ronnie's and Bubba's little sister. They also were trying their best to help the mama and daddy straighten up their lives. When one parent seemed as if they were getting better, then the other would get worse. It's so sad to see what drugs and alcohol can do to a person. People will sell their kids, their bodies, and even steal for one more bottle or one more fix. As time went on the mama signed the kids over to C.P.S. and gave up her rights.

The daddy's mama came out of the woodwork or out from under a rock (I couldn't figure which) and decided she would raise the kids. We were hearing all kinds of ugly things about her. C.P.S. conducted a home study and disqualified her as a suitable adult to raise Ronnie and Bubba. The incest accusations were so prevalent that I asked her about it. She ask if a certain person told me about it, and I assured her that my information came from another source. She said I was bound to be getting it from that person because she was the only person down here that knew about her incest. The thought of it gave me the creeps. She's not someone that I'd like to call Grandma. Months went on as our love grew for these two little boys.

The grandma didn't give up, and it was a challenge for her. She told me her other children wouldn't allow her to be around their kids so she needed these boys in her life. Eventually she threatened to get a lawyer and start a legal battle. During this time C.P.S. discovered that one of their case workers was involved in some wrong doings surrounding the kids. In their attempt to fix the problem, and not wanting the grandma to make waves, their attitude changed regarding her.

Suddenly, overnight, Grandma's home study passed. They had found her to be a suitable adult to raise our boys. It was a very sad day for all of our family. We were so scared for their future. I explained to the Grandma that

Bubba had Attention Deficit Disorder (A.D.D.) and needed help, like counseling and medication as he got older. She assured me she took him to her M.D. and he said Bubba looked healthy to him. We were told by C.P.S. that they would keep up with the boys and let us know how they were doing. Since we were still kinda new at this, we counted on the more experienced foster parents for advice. They told us the pat answer for every kid after they leave is, "They are doing fine" and they try to leave the impression that they are so happy in their new environment. How sad that C.P.S. thought we were all so ignorant. We knew they hadn't changed overnight and turned into Beaver Cleavers.

About a year and a half later we heard through their kin folks that they were dressed like rag muffins. Bubba was expelled from school for two weeks for demolishing three classrooms. They said this wasn't the first time for such behavior.

MISTI

Just when we thought God had stopped making girls, we received another call from C.P.S. They had a little girl for us. I got into "Big Red" (our van), and made the short trip to the C.P.S. office. When I got there a little boy ran to me and grabbed me by the legs and said, "I'm ready." What a cutie, rowdy and rough, but still a cutie. I mouthed to the home developer, (the cushion between all foster parents and the C.P.S. staff), that I was told we were to have a girl. They helped gently unwrap the little boy from my legs and I hugged him and assured him that his foster parents would be here soon. He bought it.

Then I saw Misti, 15 months old and just the opposite of Bubba, her brother. She was quiet and kinda bashful. No telling what fears this little darling was feeling as she and I took off for her new home. I found out there were siblings that were all going in different directions. Misti was small built, dirty, and acted hungry, so we fed her a bite and fixed a big bubble bath. She had started getting real comfortable with us by now. We gave her new clothes and she acted as if it was the very first time she had gotten anything brand new. She was a happy, pleasant child.

Misti didn't stay with us long because the foster parents that took the little boy who wrapped his arm around me when I picked up Misti at the office didn't have any children and were willing to take her so the brother and sister could be together. We agreed and knew she was going into a good, safe place. It was working out great for the kids and foster parents who were interested in adopting a little boy and girl. Every time I saw these two little children it was hard to believe they were the same kids. Now they had manners, love, and class. They made me proud. This family did a great job of molding these little urchins into a couple of model children.

As the year went on, C.P.S. turned the two little darlings back over to their birth families. Bad mistake! As time went on C.P.S. received referral after referral (calls of bad reports) trying to get help for the four kids. Finally C.P.S. was embarrassed enough that they picked them up again. At least two of the four situations had a very good ending. One of the foster parents adopted Misti and another foster couple adopted her sister. Two out of four is not bad in our business.

PAUL

One foster parent described herself as always feeling pregnant because she knew she was going to have another baby but never knew if it was a boy or a girl. Our next birth was a little boy. The nice investigator brought him to us late one night. We still had Ronnie and Bubba so now we had three little boys, ages three, 16 months, and an eight month old named Paul.

Our Paul was a skinny, little, dirty fellow. We were told that a policeman had to go into the house where Paul was laying in bed with his drunk uncle. We didn't feel that there was deliberate abuse, even with the cigarette burn on Paul's neck. We thought that the drunk uncle laid the cigarette down and little Paul, being such a fragile and weak baby, couldn't move his body. He was very neglected and gave us a faint smile as we bathed him up and got on some new pajamas. He really shined and we knew we were going to love this undernourished darling.

We realized that Paul thought he would catch up on all the food that he had been deprived of, within three weeks. We had to either slow him down or buy a herd of cows. He finally slacked off a little, realizing that he could still have more food the next day.

He thrived on being cuddled, talked to, and played with, especially when he had a full stomach, a clean body, and fresh clothes. We had ourselves a winner. He wasn't much of a noise maker, but a rather quiet baby who just enjoyed watching the circus atmosphere that was always prevalent in our home. All the laughter, yelling, crying, throwing, jumping and everything else that goes on within a family was pure entertainment for Paul. Although he was very quiet, his uniqueness surfaced, in the midst of all of our activities, with his singing at nap time and later in the evening. He would just sing so sweetly, and seemed to relish in his new found safe, and secure, place of comfort. I was the first one to hear him sing and tried to spread the news to an unbelieving family. Proof came one night when I taped him singing in his room.

He didn't need or want an audience. The tape proved that we had another Elvis on our hands. Ronnie and Bubba left us and this made Paul an only child for a while.

Reggie, our son-in-law, was stationed with the Army in Eatontown, New Jersey. We thought this would be a good time to visit with Reg, Julie Anne, and the grand boys Bubba and Buddy, since we would be traveling with just one kid. We packed and pulled out ready to see the world, or at least a little of it. We bought Big Red second hand and it already had a TV/VCR in it. This was a real blessing to us and the kids. They loved to vote on what videos they would watch and sing along everywhere we went. We were so grateful that God provided a way for us to have Big Red. So we had plenty of our kid videos fixed for Paul as we traveled hour after hour.

Along the way, we stopped at a Cracker Barrel restaurant. As Sarge and I were putting some meat on our bones, Paul started laughing real loud for our quite one. We found his source of joy when we looked at the elderly lady at the next table who was playing with him. The poor woman either had no teeth or wasn't wearing them. She and Paul were in a world of their own and enjoyed each others company.

Paul laughed, slept, talked, watched videos, ate, and cried little. What a great traveler. We had a great time with our loved ones and drove back from New Jersey in the "great blizzard of '93."

By now, Paul's birth mama was visiting with her son about every other week. His aunt had a home study conducted on herself and tried to get custody. She failed, so we enjoyed him even longer. The mama didn't know who the daddy was so we didn't have to deal with a father. As time went on, the mama didn't want to fight for him, so her rights were terminated. C.P.S. gave her every opportunity to make a life for herself and Paul. By this time the mama was expecting another baby. When we asked who the daddy was, she said, "It could be the guy that delivers cokes, or it could be that guy that works at the service station, or the neighbor." After we tried to pinpoint the daddy to be, we found out she didn't even know two of the guys by name. So another of America's children will be fighting for his or her life in a few months. So sad.

Next it was time to adopt out our quiet, little, sweet, Paul. We prayed and hoped for just the right couple to raise this special little boy. C.P.S. called and asked if we could bring him up to the office so that the adoption people, and all the other people involved could look him over, and see what a doll he was. They said we were going to help them choose just the right parents for him. We put his "Sunday go to meeting" clothes on him, and he did look good. After we shared thoughts of what we all felt was best for Paul, a lady came in and handed me a little booklet and said, "These will be the new parents." I asked if she meant this was one of the few? She said no, these are the ones she had decided on. I spoke to the lady that told me that we were to be part of the selection process. She apologized and said it was her fault because she forgot to tell the other lady that we'd be there to help choose the new parents. I believed her then and I still believe her now. We all make those kind of mistakes. The choice they made was great. Even if we had been the ones to choose, we would probably have chosen this couple to take over our job. They had a little girl one year older than Paul who born on the same date. She was left in front of a hospital and the birth mama was never located.

We started our get to know you visits. The parents came over to our house so they could meed Paul on his own turf. They all hit it off real fast. We had about two months of get together before it was time for our sweetie to go to his new home to live. We started slowly weaning ourselves away, and felt real good about Paul's future. We stayed in contact, and loved hearing from him as he developed into a Houston Rockets fan. He wore the clothes, went to the games, and watched them on TV. He and his new sister would laugh, fight, cry, and play together. This was a real satisfaction to us.

EDDIE

Late one evening we had a call from the hospital from our home developer. She had a little four month old boy for us so off I went in Big Red to the hospital. I was met with a mama and daddy crying, and grandparents trying to find out why the doctors had called C.P.S. We discovered that the young couple brought their little boy to the emergency room because he seemed to be hurting, wouldn't stop crying, and they didn't know what to do. The mama and daddy lived next door to the baby's grandparents. Daddy was out of work, and mama worked at fast food places. The daddy kept the baby while mama worked.

The hospital took x-rays and found that little Eddie had broken ribs and a broken ankle. The young daddy admitted he had been kinda rough with him but didn't mean to hurt him. They put a cast on his broken ankle, and we were told how to take care of his cast, and when we would be able to remove it. It was hard to get his little clothes over that big clumsy cast. He was a handsome little boy, and a sweeter child never lived. He just accepted everything that happened to him. He blended into the family fast, and seemed content, without pain. We knew we would see his folks at times, as we went to doctor appointments. My heart went out to this little couple that was having such a hard time in their life. I felt they loved their baby but had let all the stress of the lack of work and money, as well as living off of his parents, and a crying baby get to them. They went to court and the grandparents fought their daughter-n-law for custody of Eddie. The husband changed sides and told the judge that his wife was a good mama. The judge awarded Eddie to go his mother. The couple separated. I met the daddy in the elevator that same week. He hugged me and cried and said how he appreciated all that Sarge and I had done for his son. He was taking parenting classes and every other class he could in order to get his family back together.

MATTHEW

We received a call from C.P.S. about a little girl and her two and one half year old brother. The couple that was trying to adopt them were abusing and mistreating the little boy. We immediately picked up Matthew and Rae. They were both fairly clean and she was a little pudgy. Both kids were very good looking children. The hopeful parents had big plans of adopting them, but after having them for a while decided they didn't care much for Matthew. He appeared frightened at first when we got home, and didn't know what we would do to him. It was obvious to us that Matthew was expected to give Rae any toys that she wanted to play with, even if he had them first. He had to get her permission to play with the toys. If she didn't want the toy, then he would get to play with it. How sad. It didn't take us long to make some changes in this way of sharing. Rae didn't care for our way of letting him be part of the family, but it didn't take her long to find out her brother could be fun as a play buddy, instead of her slave.

We knew Matthew was only going to be with us a day or two because he was being sent off to Florida, to be adopted out with a couple that really did want him. The C.P.S. aide was supposed to pick him up the next morning to go to the airport. I dreaded it for this little fellow that had already been into so many different situations in his young life.

The next morning, as I opened the door, I was so thrilled to see Linda, our home developer, standing there. She said she kept thinking about Matthew all night, about all the strangers in his life. When he was picked up by C.P.S., they were strangers to him. They took him to the office, and he met more strangers. When we picked him up, he saw more strangers. Then a stranger would take him to the airport to meet a stranger from Florida to take him to his new parents who are also strangers. Now you can see why I was so grateful for such a caring and thoughtful home developer. She asked me if I would drive down to the airport with them, and I gladly accepted. Matthew and I had already became good friends so it was real pleasant for all three of us. Florida C.P.S. did well by sending a male caseworker to pick up our little fellow. The caseworker told us how anxious, and excited, the new adoptive parents were about their new child.

RAE

Rae, Matthew's sister was a pretty, dark haired girl. She had not been abused at all and had been treated like a princess. It didn't take her long to feel comfortable when she saw the playroom at our home. She didn't smile much and was quiet. We were told that she was spoiled and wasn't deprived of anything. She was so opposite of her brother. He dropped a toy once and big tears came into his eyes, so I asked him what was wrong. He pointed to the toy on the floor as if he expected to be in big trouble for accidentally dropping it. He'd just look at food but wouldn't touch it until he was told he could eat. He was scared to make a move without permission, whereas Rae had been taught that she had control over him. She was not afraid of us or anything else. It took us a while to convince her that God hadn't put her here to be in charge of the world. She mellowed out as time went on. She had a bad habit of asking for money. She would asked us, or even strangers, then try to feel for money in our pockets. We thought we had this battle won and that she understood it wasn't nice to ask for money. Then it was time for a family visit.

We dressed her up pretty and took her up to see the couple that was trying to adopt her. She was glad to see them. I couldn't believe the first question that the family asked her, "Do you want some money?" The poor baby was being taught the wrong values. It was so hard for me to see how they could be so concerned and loving to her, without even asking about Matthew. You would think they would at least be concerned that we had adopted him out or that he was no longer in our home. They had no idea that he wasn't even in Texas anymore.

Rae started to really accept our way of living. She became sweeter and enjoyed going to Sunday School. She loved dressing up and she could do a great job of dressing herself and looking like a model. She began to smile a lot more and would even give us a good laugh now and then. She made us love her slowly. It wasn't her fault that her brother was put down, in order to build her up. She didn't know better but was taught that's the way it was.

Time came for her to move and it saddened us to know that C.P.S. put her back in the same home that we took her out of. They said they couldn't prove that this family had abused her. To me, it would be enough that they had abused her brother.

MIMI

The call came one late evening for us to get a little girl from another county. We were to meet the case worker half way at a little hamburger establishment. We were there first and had some iced tea while we speculated on what kind of child was coming into our lives. We knew we wouldn't change the whole world but we had high hopes of changing our babies' little world.

As we noticed an attractive black lady coming in holding the hand of a little blond haired, blue eyed angel, we figured she was ours. She had just turned three years old and was a very energetic little girl. She sat in a high chair as we discussed her case. Her mama was living with a boyfriend who turned her in for physical abuse. Her name is Mimi. She was so delicate and pretty. Silly us, we thought we had a quiet child on our hands. She'd go along with the crowd and never do anything wrong. It didn't take us long to find out we had a little tiger. We started enjoying her from the beginning. She had only been around adults in her young life, so she thought she should be consulted as part of all of our decision making. She was funny and blended in fast, but thought it was her place to control and be in charge of the other children. They didn't quite agree. She was very independent and liked to look good. She loved to have pretty, clean clothes on at all times, even to play in the back yard. I guess she figured she could never tell when Hollywood might show up. Out of all of our children, she was the only one that always put her shoes on the right feet. We never had to correct her about it. One day she came to me and I was surprised to see her shoes on the wrong feet. I said, "Baby, look at your shoes." She laughed real big and said, "I know, Daddy did it." From then on it was a big joke that the kids would tell each other. "Don't let Daddy put your shoes on." They enjoyed laughing about it, even when no one was putting on shoes.

Mimi was very possessive of Sarge. If his coffee cup ran low, she was always there and counted it her job to refill it. When we would eat at Luby's Cafeteria, she always thought it a disaster if Sarge's tea glass would get low. She would scream across the restaurant, "Daddy's out of tea," while pointing real big to his glass. The tea lady would come a running. I never knew if she just thought Mimi was cute or if she wanted to shut her up.

If the other kids played with Sarge, rough housing on the floor, it wouldn't be long before Mimi would say, "You guys quit, Daddy's tired." She was being protective as well as jealous.

We had heard stories about Mimi's grandmother. As we dealt with her we found out they hadn't been exaggerated. We went for a family visit and Mimi's mama had said her mother could come. The mama always has that choice. The women had never gotten along and there were no signs that things were going to get better. The grandma tried to turn Mimi against her own mama and everyone else.

Mimi's mom didn't have much of a chance growing up. Her mother dominated her life and laid a guilt trip on her you wouldn't believe. When we arrived for the visit, the grandma's greeting to us was, "Don't you have any blankets?" I said, "Yes" and she said, "Why aren't they around this baby?" When we left our house the weather was great but it turned a little cooler by the time we got to Huntsville. I threw a sweater into the van before we left, just in case we needed it. I slipped the sweater on her before we went into the building. That's why we were surprised when the granny asked us about blankets. Of course, I didn't usually keep my three year old kids wrapped in blankets, even if it did turn cold.

Our case worker heard what was going on, and stepped in front of Granny. She told her if she had any complaints to make them to her and that Mimi was dressed great. We were so proud that the case worker took over, because I'm not much for trouble.

The grandma got into an argument with nearly everyone in the building. Before we left she asked our case worker for her superior's name and office location. After she balled out her supervisor, we were told that Granny wasn't allowed to attend any more visitations.

We were very relieved when we heard that Granny was to be out of the picture and out of our lives. That is, until we received a call the next week instructing us to bring Mimi up to the local office to visit with her grandma. I asked if our caseworker would be there and was told she was out of town, so we knew that they had buckled to pressure from Granny and they gave in to her without the knowledge of Mimi's mom or our caseworker. Meanwhile, while all the other adults were not getting along, Mimi was thriving, wanting to learn and teach new things.

Her mama and boyfriend settled their differences, and decided to get married. We were invited to the wedding. We dolled her up so she would make her mom proud. It was a sweet wedding at the courthouse, officiated by a judge. The mama had a good job. She was a likeable young woman that was caught up in a cycle of codependency. Grandparents passed down their problems to her parents, and they, in turn, passed them down to her. The cycle had to be broken so our baby wouldn't pass it on to her future children.

Drugs, alcohol, and welfare were accepted practices in all the past family. Mimi's birth mama was determined to be the one to break the cycle and give her little daughter a chance to have a good life. How proud we were of her because it wasn't easy for her to buck her own mama and grandma.

The new marriage didn't work out so the mama was on her own again. There wasn't any financial difference because she had been the only one working and making the living for the family.

We tried to encourage the mama all we could and on Mothers' Day we bought a cup for her with Mimi's picture on it. She knew we loved her child and she seemed to appreciate us taking her in church, and trying to teach her some morals.

Mimi's dimples were an attention getter. Everyone seemed to notice that pretty little face and her great big smile.

The mama finally got up enough courage to take over her own life. She asked Mimi's grandma to move out and told her she couldn't support her bad habits anymore. The move seemed to be advantageous for both women. The grandma started a better life alone, and then the visits with her daughter and Mimi were more special than before.

We let our Mimi go back to her mama and wished them a great life.

JEREMY

We picked up a little boy and his sister. Jeremy had just turned four. Loretta, his sister, was three.

Jeremy had big black eyes, a mischievous smile, pretty teeth, and curly dark hair. What a handsome little guy. He was one of the very few children we have had that was used to saying grace at meal time. This was a habit that was always done, whether we were eating out or at home. Every child became accustomed to it, and acted as if they were pleased we did it. Jeremy was so pleased he would bless the salt, pepper, napkins, etc. By the time he would finish the blessing, the food would be cold. None of the other children complained because they knew it would be their turn at the next meal.

Jeremy was also used to going to church. So many of our other kids went for the first time in their lives when we took them. You could tell Jeremy had a mother that was trying to bring him up right.

Jeremy enjoyed playing with the other kids. One time Mimi bit him and he came running to tell me, "Your dotta is hurting me."

One day we all made a Wal-Mart run. When we pulled into the parking lot Jeremy started singing, "Wal-Mart, Wal-Mart, that's our store, we have to go there because we're poor." We all laughed and enjoyed singing his song on all of our Wal-Mart runs. He wanted to please and worked at trying to get Sarge to go to his home and be his daddy there too. His little mama was trying to get her act together and get her kids back. She had made such a good start that we were pleased that she got another chance with them.

LORETTA

Loretta was a beautiful little girl with an olive complexion. She had long brown hair and pretty little earrings. She was well mannered and so sweet. She had a trusting nature so we knew she had not been treated badly.

Her mama had read a lot to her and she was always trying to take care of the other kids. She had a caring and loving personality. She would laugh at the other kids when they were clowning around, and she would try to please them when they weren't funny. She was a peace maker, and at times would get hurt by trying to interfere with some of the kids she thought were being too rough with each other.

Loretta didn't need to be corrected much because she worked at getting along with everyone. She reminded me of a small Mother Theresa.

She got to go back with her mama and we were glad for her, but sad for us.

LAWRENCE

C.P.S. called to see if we wanted two little boys and it sounded great to us. We went to the office and met Lawrence and Ryan.

Lawrence was a tall, long-legged four year old. He had braces on his teeth. His mom left him and Ryan, and his dad was put in jail on drug charges. The little boys were left for days to fend for themselves. It was about one and a half weeks after Easter when the boys were found at home, alone. They lived on Easter eggs left in their baskets, and some of them had spoiled. Lawrence went to one or two neighbors and asked for food for himself and his brother. The neighbors didn't realize the boys didn't have any adults watching over them. An aunt dropped by and saw the circumstances they were in. The dog nastied all over the house, and the left overs of a drug party, complete with needles, pipes, etc. didn't win any pages in "Better Homes and Gardens."

It's such a sad thing the way these people did when God allowed them to have two little boys, a big expensive house, fancy cars, a swimming pool, and all the extras in life. It shows that abuse and neglect comes with the rich and the poor.

Lawrence became content with us real fast, didn't ask about his mom or dad. We gave him a bubble bath and he smelled so much better afterwards. He had an advantage over the other kids because of all the toys, clothes and extras he was accustomed to. It didn't take Mimi very long to make him understand that she ran the show here. He finally gave in to her as the ruler and, after a while, I think he kinda liked it.

One time Lawrence got up on the top of the slide and yelled real loud, "I can fly, I can fly." We ran out the back door to tell him not to try his flying lessons from the slide. We weren't fast enough and it came as no surprise to us that Lawrence couldn't fly. He hit the ground pretty hard but luckily had no broken bones or bruises.

We made a Wal-Mart run and all the kids sat in their chairs with their car seats. After I turned the motor off I made my usual speech before we all trailed into the store, "Please do not ask for anything and use your manners." Everyone started piling out of Big Red and stood by me. Lawrence did not make a move to get out and I asked him what was wrong? He said, "Where are my manners?" Bless his heart, he was willing to use his manners if he could find them.

His daddy had bad mouthed their mama so much that we didn't think there was ever a chance for either of these parents to get within 30 feet of their boys. The daddy got out of jail, and the mama came back to Daddy. Daddy and mama got a lawyer and all was forgiven by C.P.S. The boys went back to their mom and dad.

RYAN

Ryan was a sweet, 18 month old boy. He had a round face, big smile, pleasant attitude, and was ready to embrace us as his new mama and daddy. Evidently he hadn't received very much attention at his other home, even when things were supposed to be going well for the family. Lawrence seemed to be the one that was important to them, so we could understand why our affection was so readily accepted by Ryan.

Ryan's claim to fame was the noise he could make that sounded just like a frog. He performed for us and realized how much attention it would bring him so after he would ribet, he would just laugh at himself. He brought himself pleasure with this talent.

We had high hopes that his mama and daddy would realize what a sweet gift God had given them, and give him a better life than they had previously afforded him.

RHONDA

Our next little darling was a five week old little girl. She was so little and dainty. We loved dressing her up real pretty and showing her off.

Her birth mama was a prostitute. She was back at her job when Rhonda was just three and one half weeks old. She gave her baby to a man she hardly knew, to babysit. The man was expecting to watch the baby for the weekend. After the mama didn't show up to get, or even check on the baby, the man wanted to get on with his life so he called C.P.S. The man was good to her and she was clean. She had no diaper rash, like so many of our babies came with. We could tell he was a caring person, trying to help another person out. We enjoyed Rhonda, and let her know how much she was wanted. Her mom never came back, so we were pleased to keep our sweet baby longer.

An aunt, (the mama's sister), was contacted while C.P.S. was hunting for Rhonda's mom. The aunt and uncle had been married for years and didn't have any children. They were thrilled with the prospect of possibly adopting Rhonda. They would visit each week for an hour and C.P.S. ran a home study on them. They were just what Rhonda needed. So our little sweet thing was adopted to her aunt and uncle. A few months later we babysat for them while they took a short trip. They all adjusted to each other very well and we were pleased to see another new family started.

RON

Next we got Ron, a 14 month old little baby who came to us from Texas Children's Hospital. Both of his arms were broken and in casts. The doctors said Ron's arms were broken in five different places. This tragedy happened over a period of months. The doctors also said that he must have been in lots of pain and anyone around him would surely know this. We found out the mother had signed a confession that she was the one abusing him.

The birth mother lived next door to her mother, Ron's grandma. Grandma was babysitting with Ron during these months that her daughter was abusing little Ron. I questioned C.P.S. about the grandma. Why didn't she take the boy to the doctor while she was watching him? I was told that I couldn't blame her, because she was not responsible for his broken bones. I figured she may not have broken the bones, but she should be responsible for getting him help. Even if it wasn't her grandchild, she should have help any child or adult that needed it.

With all the things known and unknown to us that happened in Ron's young life, he was a real sweetheart and trooper. He was glad to be where he felt safe and stayed close to us. He wasn't going to take a chance of us leaving him. We took him to the C.P.S. office weekly for a one hour visit with his mama and grandma. A few months after Ron came to live with us, we went to court to find out what the future held for him. The judge used common sense and said Ron should stay in foster care for a while. I wrote to this judge and thanked him for his decision.

We got the cast off both arms, and he gradually became a very secure and trusting little fellow. He really enjoyed being with the other kids. We enrolled him in Early Child Development Intervention. Ron needed this with his background, and he thrived in it. By this time we thought the birth mama would have been sent to the penitentiary. We knew the police had picked her up, but her folks put up bond and she was still coming for family visits.

After six more months we had another court date, and were told by C.P.S. that they were going to allow the baby to be in the grandma's custody. I couldn't believe it. The Ad Litem (childrens' lawyer) who was supposed to protect the child in the court cases.

C.P.S. told us to have Ron and his clothes ready for the next day. We realized that they already had a deal, since they wanted us there right after court. We didn't understand how they could give him right back into the arms of people that didn't protect him in the first place: We tried all we could, and begged them to give this boy a chance. Case closed.

JULIE

We received a call from C.P.S. that there was a newborn baby in Galveston that had tested positive for crack cocaine. She was three days old when an investigator brought us our little Julie. The investigator was a large, single man, who handled our Julie like she was a china doll. He cared so much for this child that he made the trip from Galveston to Conroe at 10:00 in the evening. The baby hadn't been named yet and the mama was mad at the daddy so she put her maiden name on the birth certificate.

The investigator said that Julie had a brother that he would bring to us the next day. When he brought Julie to us, he said C.P.S. didn't know where to locate him.

Julie was so tiny, but cute as a button. We took her without hesitation. We felt sorry for her because we realized it was going to be rough on her, having a mother that put her own desires ahead of her child's needs. We figured she wasn't concerned with the baby's life, since she failed to give her a name after carrying her for nine months. Each week we would ask if the mama had named the baby yet, and the answer was always no. We finally told them we would be glad to name her, and came up with Julie.

Sarge became consumed with Julie and took full responsibility of her. It was easy for him, since she stole his heart. When she would have withdrawals from the cocaine that was still in her body, he would wrap a blanket around her, real tight. There was really no way to relieve her of the pain she was having, but we tried so hard, and it broke our hearts. She gradually got the drugs out of her system, but had a low resistance to any sickness.

On a Christmas Eve, we rushed her to the emergency room. She was diagnosed with flu and pneumonia of the lungs. Our pediatrition told us to watch her very carefully that night. I think she would have had a better nights sleep, if we hadn't hovered over her every time she blinked an eye. She overcame her sickness within two weeks. Later we found out she also had a small heart murmur. The doctor said this should not cause her any trouble in her life.

None of the illnesses Julie experienced ever slowed down her appetite. She ate like her formula was going to be taken away. She turned into a little roly-poly. I sent a picture of her to our case worker, who showed it to the birth mother. The birth mother took the picture of our precious, fat baby, threw it on the judge's bench and yelled, "That's not my child. These people have switched kids on me because that kid is fat and I'm skinny." The judge was very disgusted with her reasoning, and after a while she was escorted out of the courtroom.

After Julie started walking and crawling with some speed, she lost much of her baby fat. Then, at a family visit, the birth mama finally claimed Julie as her child. It was so sad to us.

Sarge and Julie were like Siamese twins. They thought they were the only two people on earth. They laughed at each other over every silly thing. They brought such happiness to each other, and everyone around them. All the other kids and I just tried to tolerate their, "Us two will do" attitude.

She became healthier with each passing day, and a blessing to us all. Her hair got longer and thicker, and I put it in rollers every Saturday night, getting her ready for Sunday School.

Sometimes we would have five kids while Julie was in our care. She loved the crowd and the nightly rituals. We had a production line of shampooing their hair, drying them off, putting them all in their pajamas. I enjoyed the excitement of all the laughing, yelling, fighting, reading books, saying prayers, and watching them fall asleep at different times. How peaceful and content they looked, after we tucked them in for the night. However, we really knew they were just reenergizing for the next day.

We kept making monthly visits with Julie's birth parents. We realized the father's feelings when he told the social worker that he was tired and wanted to leave. He said, "If we can't have these kids back, we will just have more." They found fault with everything and everybody. They insisted that C.P.S. arrange to pick them up in time for their visits with the kids and even had the nerve to expect them to provide transportation to the store or any other place they wanted to go. As time went on, we and C.P.S. became immune to complaints. C.P.S. went beyond their requirements to the parents, and these people just kept taking advantage of the sweet workers. C.P.S. tried to give them every opportunity to be decent parents, but to no avail.

We all went to court to try to terminate the parent's rights. So many people were eager to give these children, Julie and her brother Gene, a chance in life. People came from all around the area, willing to testify for the babies.

Court lasted about a week and a half. The judge agreed with all of us and terminated the parent's rights. The parents are appealing the decision, claiming they did no harm to Julie, since she came to us straight from the hospital. Our lawyers said the mother had already done harm to Julie by taking drugs while she was carrying her.

We realized it was getting time to let our Julie go and we began to psych Gene and Julie up for the big separation. We heard about a couple that wanted to adopt our Julie. This young couple had no children, and were wanting to start their family. I sent pictures of the kids through our home developer to the prospective parents, and they loved her at first sight.

We met the couple, and the young lady and Julie actually resembled one another. Both have long, beautiful black hair, big brown eyes, and pretty faces. We could not have been more pleased with C.P.S.'s choice.

With all of our 36 children, we had none that were ready to leave us, or asked if they could go back to their parents. We are flattered that they have all felt safe with us.

We began to pack Julie's clothes, toys, and things that were accumulated in nearly three years. We knew that the time was close for our little darling to leave us. C.P.S. decided, against our better judgment, that Gene would fit in with the new family as well. The young couple gave it a chance, but were not informed of all the special needs that Gene had. At every opportunity, we shed as much light as possible for them.

The first visit with the parents to be went very well. Each consecutive visit in our home became more and more comfortable for everybody. Julie still called us Mama and Daddy. We started calling the prospective parents New Mama and New Daddy, and this went well. We talked to the kids during the week, and told them how great it was going to be for them. The new parents had two weekend visits before they came and picked up our little darlings.

A piece of our hearts always goes with each child. The kids knew they could call us on the phone, and we were always be available if they needed us. It was always hard to wean us away from the kids, but we knew it had to be done so we could go on with our lives.

The new adoptive parents were so kind to us, and invited us for a visit. Julie was doing great, and is now her daddy's hunting buddy. She will always be part of our lives.

GENE

The day after we got Julie from the hospital, the investigator brought us her brother Gene. This little fellow was two and one half years old, and looked more like a one year old. He was so under nourished. The clothes he wore smelled so bad that the odor nearly gagged us. His little shoes were about three sizes too big. They had such a sickening smell that we wondered how many times he had wet on them. He had no socks, and no change of clothes. He couldn't say words and grunted like a little animal. What a pitiful sight, but with such a handsome face. We bathed him at least three times to get the body odor off of him. He had been so neglected and seemed overwhelmed by the attention we were giving him. He made no connection with Julie. She was his three day old sister that he didn't even know existed. We discovered that they had an older sister that the grandmother was raising.

It didn't take long for little Gene to come out of his shell, and to make himself comfortable in his new home. We soon found out we had another Ronnie on our hands. From then on, Gene and our lives changed, not all for the better. His new home and life gave him a place of safety. He had clean clothes, food for the asking, kids to play with, a TV/VCR, a toy box in the playroom, and a big playground in the backyard. He got used to everything but the plentifulness of food. He must have had a fear that there wouldn't be any food for the next day. He would slip food into his bed at night, not taking a chance that he would be hungry when he woke up. We started giving him snacks during the night, to give him a more secure feeling. I know it wasn't the healthiest thing to do, but we were more concerned with his fear than his body at that time in his life. The food scare finally passed and then he seemed to expect food every five minutes. He could never get enough to eat. We called him our dispose-all. He could have a plate full of food, and before we even blessed it, he would ask for more. His body started filling out fine, and his handsome face started to have good complexion and color.

We gradually started to understand some words he would say, and he acted out his wants, to make us understand. We enjoyed his acting because he was so funny, and he would get tickled that he was entertaining us.

The birth parents bought Gene toy guns. The C.P.S. aide that brought the children back and forth for their visits in Galveston knew our rules on guns. Our children come from homes with enough violence, so the rules are the same now in our home as they were when we were bringing up our own children. Guns are to kill so we don't play with them. Neither do we play with knives, razor blades, bombs, or dynamite. We are very picky.

We could usually recognize the children that were allowed to play with guns. They were more aggressive, and less sensitive to the other children's needs and feelings.

We were in line at Poncho's Mexican Restaurant and Gene noticed a policeman ahead of us. Gene yelled7 "Is he going to kill me, he has a gun?" I assured him he was safe and the policeman carries the gun to protect us. The policeman was impressed with Gene, talked to him awhile, and gave him some stickers.

Foster parents know there are no shortcuts to raising kids, and Gene made us realize that even more. He always had an answer for us, even if he made it up, and he usually would. He could ask a question a minute. I asked him to please not pull his wagon onto the patio, and of course he did it anyway, and said the wagon told him to do it.

Gene liked things to do, and places to go every day. He had energy you wouldn't believe. I wish I could have bottled it and sold it. One morning as we were all getting up for the day he asked, "What are we going to do today?" I told him we were behind on so many things and we were going to have to play catch-up that day. He got so excited and yelled, "This is going to be fun playing with catsup."

He was playing in the backyard, and said he needed a stick to kill the bats. I told him that God made the bats and He loved them too. Gene said he wanted to kill the bats so they wouldn't bite God. The kids played with big rubber balls in the backyard. One time Gene took one of the balls away from the other kids, and threw it as high into the air as he could. I scolded him, but fast thinking Gene said, "I was just letting God have His turn."

I explained to him that little Julie will someday be a big girl, and that at one time he was a little boy. His question to me was, "Were you a baby Mama?"

He was being too rough with the other kids, and I asked him to please be careful, and not hurt them. He hurt one child and made him bleed. His concern was, "Where does the blood live in our body?" Gene was our one person entertainment committee, and had to be watched at all times.

When he turned three we enrolled him at Head Start School. We were all so excited because they sang his praises, and sent notes home saying how good he was doing. We were so proud that this was working out for him. Our bubble was soon popped when the notes started changing from satisfaction to terror. He began to make lots of people miserable at school. We received notes that he kicked a teacher, hit a bus driver, or spit on someone else. He became the talk of the school.

At home we seemed to be in control most of the time. He played hide and seek, and not thinking he was giving away his hiding place, he yelled loudly, "Where's me?" He knew the rules of the swing set and asked, "Can Daddy swing me way too high?"

Sarge and I had an unwritten rule that whoever got to leave the house had to take at least one kid along with us, preferably the rowdiest. When Gene and I went to the store together, we had to stop at signal lights along the way. There was an electronic signal for pedestrian crossings. The picture of a man walking was the signal for pedestrians to cross the street. I explained this to him and he wanted to know why the women and children couldn't walk?

I always told the kids that Daddy was the boss, especially when I wanted him to make a decision on something. When Gene asked me if he could do something, I asked him who the boss was and he said, "Daddy." I asked him who is Daddy's boss and he said, "God and Uncle Reggie." Although we think our son-in-law is very special, we haven't put him on the same level as God, yet.

One morning Sarge was sitting out in the carport with the kids, waiting on the school bus. Gene slipped back into the house, locked them out, and started watching TV. He wouldn't let them in and didn't want to catch the bus.

We would be foolish enough on rainy days to take the umbrella to the bus stop to protect them from the rain until they got inside the house. Once inside, they headed out the back door to play in the rain. We wasted a trip.

It was the same idea when we asked them to pick up the trash in the yard. They said, "It's too hot." Then we saw them running real fast and playing ball. Evidently, a quick cold spell came in on us.

At school, Gene loved to play with the "puter," as he called it. He really was good with computer work and we encouraged him all we could.

The kids got out of school for Martin Luther King JR.'s birthday. Gene wanted to know what we were going to get him for his birthday.

As time went on my mama's signs of Alzheimer Disease got worse and we knew we needed her to move in with us, so we could take better care of her. She loved the kids and they loved her. It was a special need they all had.

She didn't realize that she accidentally scared them at times. At night before I tucked them into bed, she would tell say, "Night, Night, sleep tight, don't let the bed bugs bite." They had this big fear that there were bugs in their beds. Mama also didn't realize that most of our kids had never been rocked before they came to live with us. So some of our babies didn't appreciate the song about, "Rock-a-by-baby when the cradle will fall, down will come cradle, baby, and all."

One night Sarge and I had our own production line of shampooing their hair, bathing their bodies, and putting on their pj's. I could tell that Sarge was about at his wits end. We had five little ones and we were down to our last baby when I told Sarge real softly, "When we get the babies in bed we will have some P-I-E." Like a flash from his room, Gene came running down the hall yelling, "I want some P-I-O." He didn't know what it was but he knew if I spelled it, it must be good. So from then on we always called pie, P-I-O.

Gene begged me to make P-I-O at least every other day. He loved to help me roll out the pie crust, and watch it turn brown in the oven. I'd put the timer on, and every time it dinged he would say, "Lets cook it two more minutes." He got this from the first time he helped me with the baking. I'd said it's not done so we'd bake it another two minutes. He figured this was a lifetime cooking procedure.

He also loved chocolate chip cookies and knew I'd save him at least eight little chips for him to eat. This was always a special treat that he would expect any time he smelled cookies baking. If he came in from school and I'd already baked the cookies, he would run to the little cup where he knew I'd put his eight chocolate chips.

A friend of ours died and I made a P-I-O to send to the family. Gene got excited when he saw the P-I-O, but was very disappointed when I told him we were sending it to my friends. He said, "I do not want that dead man eating my P-I-O." I told him it was for the family and that the dead man couldn't move or eat.

A lady in my Sunday School Class was nice enough to come by and pick up the P-I-O to take to our mutual friend. When my friend got here, Gene assured her he wasn't dead and he could eat the P-I-O, if she would leave it.

The next morning, on our way to church, I commented that there was a dead chow dog on the side of the road. I was trying to make a point to the kids that the chow wouldn't have gotten hit by a car if he had not been in the road. Nothing else was said about the dead dog until we got out of church. The first thing Gene said was, "Lets go see about that dead chow dog." On the way home we slowed down so Gene could see what happens to animals who play in the road. He looked so serious and said, "Boy, that dead chow's not going to be eating any P-I-O."

Sarge's brother died and we went to the funeral parlor and service. Gene wanted all the details, since we didn't take him with us. We tried not to dwell on death but wanted to be honest, emphasizing Heaven. He said his biggest worry about dying was not knowing what to do with his hands in that box. I assured him that the people would take care of that for him, and he shouldn't be concerned about it. He said he needed to talk to God before he goes to Heaven, to be sure God has a real good playroom for him.

Gene's little helper was a blond one year younger than him named Anne. They made a team. One night Sarge made the mistake of leaving his camera on the kitchen table. It's kinda fancy and winds automatically at the snap of a picture. We woke up the next morning and noticed that the camera had been moved. We asked Gene and Anne if they had touched the camera. In unison we heard a real strong, "No sir" from both of them. We had the film developed, and I wish you could have seen them. One picture was of the top of Gene's head, one was of Anne's feet, and one was of the ceiling light. They went all through the house taking pictures of everything they liked, including the toy box. They had no idea that developing the film would expose them. When we showed them the pictures, Anne said, "Him did it," and Gene said, "Her did it." Such fond memories as we look back at the pictures today.

I got Gene help from psychiatrists, psychologists, and any counseling that I hoped would help him. He could be in trouble with everyone and I'd try talking to him, explaining how important it was to not beat people up, slap, hit, kick, spit on, trip, or be unkind at all. I would be in the middle of my lecture and he would put his arms around me and say, "I'll always be your darling" and I would always agree. I'll love him forever.

It was time for his sister Julie to be adopted. I asked C.P.S. to please wait on Gene's adoption because he definitely was not ready.

We went to the doctor to get physicals on the kids. It was mainly for our benefit, feeling safer knowing it was on record that they were in good health and had no bruises, cuts or broken bones. We never wanted it to come back some day that they had been abused while in our care.

The doctor gave a complete physical by checking Gene from head to toe. I thought everything was going ok until the doctor finished Gene's checkup and sat down. Little Gene looked real hard at the doctor and said, "That wasn't nice what you did to me" and the doctor said, "What did I do?" Gene said you touched my private parts. The doctor looked at me for help. I told Gene I was pleased that he called him on it and it was ok this time, since Mama was there. I also told him that I was proud that he spoke up and knew it wasn't acceptable at other times. The doctor called Julie over and was fixing to check her throat and teeth. Just before he touched her mouth, my little Gene blurted out to the doctor, "Aren't you going to wash your hands?" The doctor jumped up and said, "Of course," because he knew we all realized he had just finished Gene's physical. I was so proud of Gene that he kept the doctor in line without being disrespectful. It gave me the creeps, knowing that after he finished examining Julie, he left our little room without washing his hands. Then he went into another child's room to pass germs from one kid to another.

As the time got nearer, I talked to everyone that would listen to me to beg them not to adopt Gene out yet. Their reasoning was that he needed to be with his sister. No one feels stronger than me that siblings should not be separated, but there are exceptions. Julie would not have a good life as long as Gene's with her. Gene takes all of your time and emotions, and you would be so worn out by the time you get around to giving Julie just a little of your attention and time. He demands the center of attention at all times.

Sometimes we are much closer to friends than blood kin. I don't feel we should ruin a child's life just to say we are keeping siblings together.

C.P.S. said the same couple that wanted to adopt Julie wanted to adopt Gene too. Again I asked if they would just please wait until the psychological reports on Gene came back, so we could show the adoptive parents what they would be up against. After all, this is their life too. They needed to be told much more than he was just a handful. Every one of our foster kids have been a handful. They need to know the facts about what they are getting into.

The people that wanted to adopt Julie and Gene were a precious little couple. We started psyching the kids up for the big move. We started calling the couple their "New Mama and New Daddy." I turned it over to God, and knew he was still in charge.

We had only two weekend visits before the children moved in with their new parents. They left on Thursday, and the adoption coordinator called on Monday, saying that the couple had decided against adopting Gene, but still wanted to adopt Julie. We didn't blame the little couple at all because we had lived with Gene for three years, 24 hours a day. We knew and understood why it was not working out. They said that after dealing with Gene they were emotionally and physically wasted, and they had nothing left for Julie. They were wise to see this early, before C.P.S. closed the book on the case, like they are so famous for. At first we didn't feel like we could take Gene back into our lives again, because we needed a break from him as much as we loved him. After talking it over we knew we wanted him back, so we called C.P.S. the next day. The caseworker was determined to show us she was going to put him into another foster home in another city, away from us, and away from the adoptive parents. She must have felt guilt for rushing into the adoption, after I begged her not to. Then, when the couple didn't work out, she let her pride over rule Gene's care by not letting him come back home, where he told them he wanted to be.

The caseworker told me she was taking the legal papers over to the new foster parents to sign. I told her we needed him back because we had him under psychiatric care, and he needed more help. I'm sure the new foster parents were nice people and good parents, but our caseworker was trying to blame others when it was her decision not to do what was best for the child, and her guilt would affect the life of our little boy.

From then on we knew there was no need to ask about him, because we would get the same answer all the foster parents get after the kids leave, "They are doing fine." It always amazes me how a child, overnight, can turn from a misfit into a sweet little choir boy.

This was about the time in my life that I was tempted to go out and get a job so I could get some rest. I decided instead to go to the doctor, and see why my arm and hand was hurting so much. After x-rays, the doctor said that I needed a leave. Boy, was I sure that I went to the right doctor. My mind started to fantasize about a trip by myself to just sleep, sleep, and sleep some more. I assured him he had prescribed the magic words, but I just didn't know how I could take a leave right now. Then he hit me with a bombshell and let me know he meant the medication, "Alieve." I nearly went into a deep depression, thinking they would consider putting me in the Intensive Care Unit. That didn't work either. The doctor assured me I just had arthritis, and I'd live through it all. He told me to go home and count the one hour visit in the doctor's office as a coffee break.

MIKE

We received a three month old little boy from the Texas Children's Hospital. He came to us neglected and abused. He had no desire to thrive. He had a rash all over his little body, especially around the diaper area and his neck. He was very uncomfortable. We had to take special care to relieve him of as much pain as we could. He was a sweetie, and didn't cry much. I guess he became accustomed to feeling bad.

He began healing fast, and became a very pleasant little baby. We kept some very strong ointment on him, and his complexion started to look like it should have from the beginning.

We really could not find a lot of abuse. There was possible neglect by not changing his diapers enough, and not doctoring his rash. Neglect is a form of abuse, so maybe the little mama learned her lesson. Most of the problem seemed to stem more from ignorance than anything. She hadn't been taught how to take care of her baby. She was willing to take parenting classes. Mike started to thrive, and looked very good when we returned him to his little mama. She was so excited to get another chance, and I'm glad she had it.

RAY

We received a call about 2:30 Sunday morning. There was a mother threatening to jump off of a building, and take her baby with her. The police talked her down, and got the baby from her. We found out she had a history of mental problems. C.P.S. already had her other child in the system. Ray didn't seem to be mistreated, and the mama volunteered to put him in our care, because she realized she couldn't care for him.

He was a very strong baby, and seemed to be normal in social and developmental skills. His mom and dad had both been in and out of mental hospitals, and were both seeking help. Some of our foster parent friends had Ray's brother, so everybody concerned was in one accord, thinking it was best for Ray to be placed with his brother. The transition went smoothly, so we were all pleased to see him go with our friends. A couple of years later these foster parents adopted Ray and his brother. Happy ending.

SUNNI

This was a sad case for us. They brought Sunni to us one evening. She looked like a Gerber baby, so round with fat cheeks. She was five months old. I dressed Sunni and Julie like twins. They looked adorable and played well together. The older kids always referred to them as "their baby girls." We got Sunni because of the abuse that was given to her brother Michael. He was taken away from his mother because her husband broke both of his legs and arms. Thank goodness they got Sunni out of the situation. We were keeping up with Michael's progress through his foster parents. He bonded with his new family very quickly. Until now, he had had such a horrible little life. As in so many of our cases, the birth parents will not care for one of their children, blaming everything on the one they feel that's bringing bad things into their lives. The other children in the house are taught that this bad child is a free target for everyone.

Our little Sunni wasn't abused, so we had ourselves a healthy, beautiful child. We enjoyed her so much, and thought maybe, because of her brother' s severe abuse, we would get to keep her until she went to college.

The birth mother's husband went to jail for abusing Michael. This pleased both sets of foster parents. Months passed as Sunni became more bounded with us. She was a sweetie.

Michael's foster parents contacted us about going to court. The birth mama wanted her kids back, although it was proven that she had never protected her children. She was suspected of being part of Michael's abuse at times.

The lady district attorney gave it all she had. Both sets of foster parents begged the court to read the background, and check into the past records of these abusers. The judge had one thought, and one thought only, and that was to reunite the family.

During this time our caseworker changed, and the new one would not listen to anyone, and she let the birth mama con her.

I contacted the head honcho at C.P.S., trying to get our babies some help. She looked into it and agreed with us, but the judge had already made his ruling. Consequently, two more children were lost in the system, and not given a chance.

We all knew the husband was supposed to get out of jail real soon, and the birth mama made no bones about taking him back, and having her family together again. Bad move.

CLETA

One evening we were called to pick up a sister and brother team. Cleta was five years old and Mark was two. From the beginning we knew this little girl had problems, and would need lots of help.

Cleta was what we call a head banger. As her emotions got stronger, she more intensely slammed her head backwards. I thought the poor little thing would break the van chair on our way back to the house that evening. As we came in, she began to settle down, and by the time she saw the toys, she was pretty calm, cool and collected.

Our babies have called their grandparents every name in the book from Granny, Gramgram, Gram, Mimi, Mawmaw, Grandmaw, Gams, Moo-Moo, Mee-Maw, and Grandmother. We were surprised when Cleta called for a lady's name. Then we realized it was her grandmaw's. She was the only one we ever had who called her grandmother by her first name.

As we drove into our church parking lot the next morning, Cleta said, "This is where I go to church." I thought maybe she was confused, since lots of churches look similar. I soon discovered that she was right.

One of our church members greeted our Cleta, and let me know he was one of her grandparent's neighbors. I was so pleased to know she had these good grandfolks to fall back on. Soon I found out that the grandparents were interested in raising the children and keeping them active in church. How pleased I was.

At the house Cleta started to fit in very well. She loved all kinds of Indian thing. Pocahontas was her favorite.

She loved playing in the backyard. She would swing real high for at least 15 minutes straight. She had symptoms of Fetal Alcohol Syndrome. She really needed lots of counseling. She was sexually molested by her stepfather many times. She went through a lot, so no wonder she was such a nervous child. She gradually began to enjoy laughing, and playing hard with the other children.

She has a speech delay, but with treatment that can all be improved. The grandparents fought to get their grandchildren and we were glad they won. The grandparents threw a big welcome home party for their new family they would raise. Neighbors, kin, and all other loved ones came to share the joy. They probably cooked the fatted calf. Good move.

MARK

We picked up little Mark, two years old, with his sister Cleta. He was a quiet, shy little boy. I'm sure some of this was out of fear. This was a big deal for him. None of our kids ever know what they are getting into. They aren't sure if it's going to be any better than what they have been taken out of.

Little Mark had a pierced earring on, and needless to say he lost it the first night. We had two little boys with earrings. It wasn't long after we got home that Mark took his place in my lap to be rocked. He was just in for the ride, since he was picked up because of the sexual abuse of his sister. C.P.S. knew that Mark needed to be taken out of that situation, so, as in many other cases, they made a good judgment call. Mark liked all the loving we gave to him. He liked to be held, liked to talk, and could say lots of words. He was a cutie. He was in for a treat to be raised by his grandparents. They are into ranching and have some acreage in the county. We felt very good about this situation.

JUSTIN

Justin came to us with a failure to thrive. This was due to his parents not providing for his developmental and emotional needs. He had a bad diaper rash and was a case of neglect. His mother's mental condition wasn't that great, and the father was so absorbed in himself that their children didn't have much of a chance.

We took him for his weekly, one hour visit with their parents. When I picked Justin up, the dad was always sprawled out (all 350 lbs.), sound asleep on the couch. The mother sat on the floor, playing with the toys. Justin seemed to be trying to take care of them. He and I were both glad to get out of there and home again.

The parents didn't appear too eager to get Justin back. They kinda enjoyed everyone else taking care of him — buying him clothes, feeding him, and providing for all of his needs.

Justin started to thrive. He loved laughing, standing up in the play pen and yelling at us for attention. He was a sweet little darling. He improved so much that C.P.S. thought it was time for his parents to take back their responsibility. We didn't think that the parents had advanced as much as Justin. We suggested that the folks should get more parental training. Our suggestion was ignored and Justin went back to his home. Eight months later we heard that one of the C.P.S. ladies visited in their home. She saw roaches running all over Justin's face and body. This didn't seem that unusual to the parents. They had not improved on caring for

Justin at all. He was finally placed back into foster care and I heard that C.P.S. was recommending termination of the parent's rights. That was good news. Our baby will finally have a decent chance at life.

KAREN

Late one night around midnight, I met an investigator in front of our C.P.S. office. She had a little baby girl, four months old. I wish you could have seen her that night, you would have been taken just like I was. She had big blue eyes, and just a little fuzz for hair. Her mom said, "I have no job, no money, no food, no house." This was the best thing she could think to do for her baby. It sounded so bad for a mom to give up her child. However, the ones that complained the most weren't willing to lift a finger to help her. I thought she was showing love for the child by giving her to C.P.S., knowing that she would be well taken care of. The next morning the mom showed up with Karen's birth certificate and after signing her rights away, we were smitten with this little precious one. There wasn't a father on the scene, or any other kin that we knew of.

A few days later we heard that some of our foster parent friends wanted to adopt a child. Karen seemed to be just what God had sent them. We made arrangements for this young, childless couple take our Karen. They, as well as the C.P.S. workers, were so excited when we took her, in her, "go to meeting clothes" to the office to make the transition. We took video of the prospective mama and daddy getting to see their little girl for the first time.

Everything was going beautifully in the new family's life. Their church gave them a baby shower and Karen got to meet all her new grandparents, aunts, uncles, cousins, and neighbors. Then the shocking news. A grandmother had just heard that her grandchild was being given away. What a heart break for everyone concerned. The adoption papers hadn't been signed because of the mandatory waiting period. A home study was done on the grandmaw and she didn't meet the criteria. By this time Karen's newlywed father heard that he was her daddy. With this news he set out to get custody of his daughter. By this time our friends had gotten over the shock of their lives being turned upside down.

Our friends loved Karen so much and were allowed to keep her for about 13 or 14 months. They gave her a wonderful start in life and graciously accepted the birth daddy and his new wife taking over their responsibilities. They had done such a good job raising Karen. They are now in the process of adopting two more little girls that are in foster care. We wish them the best of everything, they deserve it.

REGGIE

We got Reggie and Mikey because of drugs in their home. Reggie was three years old, and cute as a button. He came in with a bang. I don't think he was ever uncomfortable. He made himself at home immediately. We felt like we were renting the house from him. He was so used to being left with strangers, that he wanted it clear from the beginning that he was in charge. He was so precious and funny. He loved everything and everybody. He was so easy to please. He was impressed with the bubble bath and clean clothes. He hadn't previously known anything about cleanliness, so it was just like Christmas every day for him.

In Sunday School, on Mother's Day, he made me a little hand print of plaster paris, and was so excited about giving me his gift. I thought I'd cry when he waited until we got home from church, and took his little hand print out of his gift wrapping. He said, "Mommy, I made this for you cause I love you." He loved giving. The other children, acting just like kids, started asking Reggie for their handprint gift. He pointed at each of the other kids and said, "I'm going to make you one, and you one, and you one, and you one." Then he looked up at Sarge and said, "Daddy, I'm going to make your Mother's Day handmark, too". We really enjoyed this little boy.

Reggie loved playing outdoors. He could play with the roughest of them. He visited his birth mom every week for one hour. However, he showed no emotion. He was more impressed with the toys in the visiting room than in seeing his mother. Concluding the visit, he always said, "Lets get home Mommy." He never lost his enthusiastic outlook on life. He protected the other kids, and was also a peacemaker. He didn't like anyone being unhappy, and felt it was his place to make them glad.

With great sadness, we heard that C.P.S. was fixing to give the kids back to their drug crazed birth parents. We protested this move as much as possible. It was obvious to nearly everyone how unwise it was to send the kids home.

We were so pleased when we heard that our young investigator was gathering information for a court case. She was trying to keep the children away from those noncaring people, posing as parents. The investigator summoned many people that had evidence of the birth parent's lifestyle, and a pattern showing there was no consideration by them, for their children. It was supposed to be brought out in court that they would leave all four of their children with anyone they could unload them on. They would ask people to watch the kids for a few hours, and not return for two or three weeks. This pattern went on from city to city. Our investigator prepared an excellent case for us.

Evidently, the ad litem (children's lawyer) and the judge had already decided that the children would be returned to their parents. It was so plain to all the foster parents, and I believe to everyone else concerned, that it would be a bad mistake to release our children back into this situation. The judge didn't give our investigator a chance to present her case or call on any of the witnesses she had subpoenaed. He made the ruling from the ad litem's case, and everyone lost.

We were told to have Reggie and Mikey at the office by 1:00 to return to their creepy parents. The other foster parents were also told to have the two siblings of our boys up there too.

When we met with the parents, I thought I was going to be sick. The father was wearing an ankle ring because he was on probation and that the authorities had to know where he was at all times. You would think his wearing the ankle ring in court would tell them something. Then I saw the huge swastika sign on his shirt. All I could think of was him raising four children to start four new families, and trying to be like the Oklahoma City bomber, Timothy McVey.

The mama told us how great it was that her children loved us so. Then the four little children went back into a troubled home life.

MIKEY

We picked up Mikey and Reggie from other foster parents. They were precious people, but had too much going on in their lives right then to take on two more little active boys. They had our boys for four days.

Mikey was a one year old child who loved to be held a lot. He possessed a quieter nature than his older brother. He soon became partners in crime with little Julie. She took him by the reins and decided to be his mama, his ruler, his boss, and his dictator. Mikey was such a good natured baby that he went along with Julie's plan. The other kids tried to stay clear of these two dynamos because together, they could destroy everything around them. They were such characters. I think they both spoke Chinese, because only they could understand each other.

After we returned Mikey to his folks, we were concerned about what would become of him. About five months after the four children were returned, we read in our local newspaper that the father was arrested in a big drug bust. It was good to know that he was finally away from the children.

One month later we read front page news that a five year old boy had been dropped off into the woods and left all night. The story said the boyfriend of our Mikey's and Reggie's mom had put the boy out of his car. He got permission from the mom to pick the child up from school. Then he took him to the edge of the woods and said, "I'll pick you up later." Of course, he was a no show. The five year old boy was Mikey's and Reggie's oldest brother. He wandered around in the woods all night, scared to death, fighting mosquitoes and other insects. As daylight came he spotted a woman out by an oil pump. The tired, scared, little boy approached her and asked if she could help him. The nice lady took the lost little boy to safety.

The birth mama told the police that she had been in the woods all night, hunting her little boy. The police asked her to show them the mosquito and other insect bites like her son had all over his body. She had none. She finally admitted that she was at a party in Houston until two or three in the morning. Understandably, the mama went to jail. This was getting to be pretty good news to us, having the father, mother, and boyfriend all in jail. We all rejoiced and hoped these low lifes would spend a considerable amount of time in jail. Meanwhile, the little boy was coming along fine with some nice foster parent friends of ours.

I asked about how the other three children were doing. This did not turn out to be a simple matter. No one knew where the other three kids were at. I asked at the C.P.S. office about them and they didn't know anything. I asked the detective that was in charge of the boyfriend and mama's case, but he hadn't even been told that there were anymore children.

I asked everyone that would listen to me, my concern growing with each month. I was in contact with Laura Bush's office (Governor Bush's wife), and she wanted me to contact the state director of the Texas C.P.S. I did that, and he sent me forms explaining that C.P.S.' main object is to reunite the family. I talked to a judge who seemed concerned, but that's as far as it went. The nice detective was giving his all, but he could only do so much. I'm sure people got tired of hearing about my concerns, but I just couldn't let it go.

I heard that they may be in a little town in Arkansas. I called everybody with their last name that was given to me. No luck. After about eight months, I decided to call the same caring lady that had helped us with one of our other babies, Sunni. She is one of the head honchos at C.P.S., and a very concerned lady. We are blessed to have her in the system. After I explained my concern about the three missing children, she made contact with our local office, and they, in turn, made contact with the C.P.S. in Arkansas. The case worker in Arkansas said all three children were living with distant kin of the birth parents. All I'd asked from the beginning was to know if our babies were safe.

KATHY

Kathy was a little sweet girl, 11 months old. She came to us from the Texas Children's Hospital and was thought to have been abused. She was a butterball with dark hair, a big dark eyed beauty. She was solid weight. She weighed as much as our two year olds. She was a sweet, lovable, little girl that had been living with her mama, uncle, and grand daddy. They all seemed to love her so much, and it was agreed finally, that she had something seriously wrong with her. It was not abuse, but a very large brain tumor that made things appear abnormal. She was taken from us, and put back into the hospital for surgery. The last I heard, little Kathy will be able to lead a normal life. It made us feel good that she was returned to her mama and family.

CLINTON

One night about 10:30 I met a C.P.S. investigator and policeman with two new children for us. Clinton was one year old and his sister Anne, was three years old.

The policeman went into the home and removed the children. The mama stabbed the daddy and Clinton was found laying in a pool of his daddy's blood. Rumor was that the daddy was H.I.V. positive. The mama went to jail, the daddy went to the hospital.

The policeman and C.P.S. investigator said these kids were suffering in horrible living conditions. Roaches were in the refrigerator and frozen in the deep freeze. Filth, cans and clutter were a foot deep throughout the entire house. When we got home that night, we found a sickening sight. We opened the suitcase that the policeman packed for the kids, and roaches scattered everywhere.

We took Clinton to the doctor and found that he had lead [*lead* written above *iron*] in his blood. We knew this could affect the rest of his life by not allowing him to learn and could possibly cause retardation These issues were extremely important to us. He was a pleasant little boy who thrived on attention, and needed love badly. As with most of our kids, Julie became his leader and they made a good team.

Clinton loved to play outdoors, and was a good little sport. We would swing him in the baby swing and he laughed during the whole ride. I was concerned about his health since he was found laying in a pool of blood. I expected them to run tests on our little fellow, but it didn't happen.

We gave Clinton a haircut and he sat as still as a mouse while his hair fell to the floor. He loved to be dressed up for church, and enjoyed cleanliness. He seemed to like being a follower instead of a leader. He believed anything Julie told him, and they held many long conversations that only the two of them understood.

We expected to have Clinton and Anne for quite a long time since their folks had so many problems. Their daddy was on probation for sexual assault. The assault was not on a child, and it happened years ago. He broke his probation when the big fight broke out with his wife. Our expectations came to an end when C.P.S. said they were going to return the children to their parents.

ANNE

Anne took the transition in stride, since she was accustomed to her mom and dad fighting a lot. She was in her pajamas the night I picked her up from the police and C.P.S. investigator. She had the most beautiful smile I'd ever seen, and her pretty teeth enhanced her beauty. She had a contagious laugh, and was such a great treat to our family.

She visited weekly with her birth parents but showed very little emotional attachment towards them. However, she showed more than her parents did towards her. We enrolled Anne into Head Start. Gene was already giving them a fit at that little school, so we felt guilty sending another one of our kids. They were not in the same classrooms. I think that was by popular demand. We never received a bad report on Anne. I suppose they were too occupied with Gene.

At home, Gene and Anne became partners in crime. They got into one thing after the other. They would laugh at each other, and be real dramatic. They became extremely close and loved each other very much.

Anne was Gene's helper and co-worker on the night of the big camera tour of our home. The two of them would play on the swing set, ride, and drive the electric Barbie car. Also, every Saturday was our Whopper run to Burger King. All the kids planned each week on the special treat of Burger King. The Whoppers were 99 cents so we could indulge the whole family without floating a loan. We would get the kids french fries, too. Buckled up in their assigned seats, the kids always loved it when we would throw them a french fry, one at a time.

The daddy had a back track record of violence, with such a bad temper. While we had the kids in custody, the daddy received a notice from the environmental inspectors to clean up his yard within 48 hours. This was sad, especially after we had heard what the inside of the house looked like. I have heard of environmentalists dealing with big companies and stores, but have never heard of a residence being so bad that they had to step in.

Our concern was growing about them being put back into their folk's care. Others became concerned too. The ad litem (children's lawyer) and CASA (Court Appointed Special Advocates) were trying to do all they could to keep the children safe.

Every one of us tried to reason with C.P.S., but to no avail. They said that the daddy was going to prison for breaking his probation. C.P.S. reasoned that with the daddy gone, the kids would be safe. Of course, we all understood that they wanted to return the kids back to the mama, and then close the case. By the time the daddy gets out of prison, C.P.S. will be out of the picture. Out of sight, out of mind. The judge was asked to intervene in this case, but he chose to ignore pleads from at least three different sources. It's so sad that he missed an opportunity to help and protect these babies.

We were told by C.P.S. that we couldn't expect these parents to change and have our lifestyle. We weren't concerned that much about changing the parents. We were more interested in protecting the children from the parent's lifestyle and were just thinking of their safety.

BUDDY

We picked up Buddy at C.P.S. because he was an abandoned three month old baby. His brother was in C.P.S. custody a few years earlier. He was a cute, healthy, fat baby.

We didn't keep Buddy long because there are rules about not having over two children less than 18 months old. He would put us over our limit with our little ones, and we still had the older children. He went to live with some of our foster parent friends.

LUKE

Our little Luke was two years old. He had long auburn hair and an earring in his pierced ear. The earring got lost the first day we had him, like it did with our boy Mark. He had beautiful hair, which was cut the next day. His developmental levels were all below par. His front teeth had been pulled out, but he had a pretty smile. He was a very neglected child. His birth mama and grandmother had been leaving him here and there since his birth. He had no security whatsoever. He was left with practically strangers for weeks at a time, without the family ever checking to see if he was being taken care of.

Luke was a slow thinker, although he was so very lovable, and could take all the attention and cuddling you could provide. He really enjoyed all the other kids and the family atmosphere. This was all new to him, and he started making progress.

Little by little we understood his language, learning it word by word. We tried to teach him new things every day.

Sarge was teaching him to shake hands when greeting someone. In one of his lessons, he gave him hands on instructions. Sarge approached Luke, held out his hand, and told him to, "shake." Little Luke started to shake his body all over. Sarge started laughing, and thought maybe he would start another, easier lesson.

Like some of our other children, we enrolled Luke in Head Start. This was great for him, and he started to blossom quickly. His words became more understandable. Sarge and I nearly understood all that he was trying to say, and we interpreted it to the other people.

When Big Red would get low on gas, we would always say, "Big Red is thirsty, he needs petro." We tried to teach our kids manners when they would burp, belch, or pass gas. We let them know it was polite to say, "Excuse me." We couldn't help but laugh when little Luke said, "Excuse me, I passed petro." And I thought it was cute one day when he saw me putting away my panty hose and kept calling them my "panty socks."

His family visits were every other week for one hour. His mom didn't show much emotion. She had given one of her other children to her mother-in-law, so in her weak mind she thought she should give Luke to her mom. It only seemed fair to her.

Our love for Luke grew, and we realized how much he needed structure in his young life. The mom's rights were terminated, and out of the blue a daddy came onto the scene. The daddy and Luke took blood tests to see if he really had fathered our little one. Sure enough, he was the one.

The daddy started working on getting custody of Luke. Luke's paternal grandmother was thrilled about having a grandson. The daddy couldn't swing it financially by himself to raise Luke, so it was suggested that he move in with his mom. Then they could help each other. The move took place, and things seemed to be going their way.

While Luke lived with us we knew he had a low self esteem. It's been said, "If you aim at nothing, you will hit it every time." We encouraged Luke to aim high. We tried to instill confidence into him. He gradually thought more of himself and accomplished things that he before wouldn't even try.

By now, we had moved my mama in with us. She was diagnosed with Alzihimers Disease. She and Luke really hit it off. They seemed to need each other. We enjoyed having "Mama Retta" with us. One time she asked if there was anything at all she could do to help, so I gave her a safety pin and rope belt to run through the waist of one of the boy's pants. She tried it about three seconds and handed it back to me and said, "That's hardly worth my time." I couldn't help but laugh at her because I knew she had nothing else in the world to do but nothing to her was much more important than doing this simple job.

Luke's dad was about to get custody of his son. Luke and Dad will live with Grandmaw. The dad took a psychological test and failed. He was not stable, and the chance was taken away from him to have primary custody. So new ways were looked at to get Luke back with his family.

The best solution seemed to let the grandmother have custody of him. His dad, with his bad temper and temptation to be in control at all times, moved out of his mom's house. He could still be in close contact with his son and visit often. This seemed to be workable for all of us, so our little auburn haired Luke went home. The grandmaw will see to it that he has a good life. She is a sweet and caring person.

LEWIS

Lewis was a 13 month old, chubby little Spanish baby. He was in good condition, but was brought into the system because of his sister and step-father's actions. His 10 or 11 year old sister and her step-father were carrying on an affair. They ran off together, and the girl's mother, (his wife), called the cops on them. The girl was found and put into foster care with her younger sister. We got Lewis, the baby brother.

One of the sad things was the silly little girl kept running away from her foster home to be with the step-father pervert. The girl claims to be madly in love with him. She said her mother was just jealous because her step-father loved her more than he loved her mother.

The young girls could speak English but the mama claimed she could neither speak or understand the language.

Lewis wore a beautiful little ivory horn necklace. He pulled the horn out of the clasp, and we put it away so he would not swallow it.

We had an interpreter during the family visits because taco and tortilla were the only Spanish I spoke. The mama, through the interpreter, asked about the horn necklace. I told her that the necklace broke and before I could explain that I'd put it away for safe keeping, she said, "It broke, what happened?" Then I said, "I thought she couldn't speak or understand English." The mama said, "I know just a few words." I guess I hit on just the few words that she knew.

Our investigator told me after the visit that the mama called her every day, spoke English, and understood everything going on.

Lewis was a sweet, happy boy who was well cared for. We enjoyed him, although he really didn't understand any of our English. The mama wanted Lewis in a Spanish speaking home, and went to a Spanish organization to put the pressure on C.P.S. They were not at fault, and tried to satisfy the Spanish group.

We didn't have Spanish speaking foster parents in Montgomery or Walker Counties. So, to appease the mama and her backers, all the children were returned to this woman. By now, the step-father had gone to Mexico, and we felt it wouldn't be long before the mama would arrange for she and the children to join him there. So sad.

JIMMY

A call came from the Galveston C.P.S. They had a newborn little black baby boy. He was three days old when we got him. This was our first black child so we had a lot to learn. He was such a joy to us. We didn't think there would be any difference in the way we would take care of him, than all the other kids we've had in our home. However, we were wrong.

The first scare came when he started to turn an ash color. I called my black foster parent friend. She was very calm and knew, from the beginning, how to help us in raising our baby. She told us to keep petroleum jelly or baby oil on him all the time. That did the trick. Another thing I learned from her is that black children do not get head lice. It has something to do with the chemicals in their hair.

When we took Jimmy out in public, people had questions about our relationship. Most people asked if he was our grandchild? If we had three or four of our children with us, people seemed to take it for granted that we were poor old people that were having to raise all their grandchildren. Then one of our babies would call us mama or daddy and the people would really feel sorry for us. They didn't realize that this was our choice.

When Jimmy was about two months old he got real sick, so we kept him in the hospital for two nights. The doctors were afraid that he had meningitis. However, all of the tests came back negative. Two months later he was sick again, and the pediatrician said he probably had asthma. We treated him accordingly, and he has turned out as healthy as a little horse, except for colds now and then.

Jimmy was one of six children. His mama has the mentality of about an 11 or 12 year old child. We are not sure if she was in an accident, had a disease that caused her illness, or was born that way. Doctors are testing Jimmy to see if any problems are inherited. So far his is doing great, and is the happiest baby we've ever had. He wakes up happy and goes to sleep happy. He has added so much to our lives with his sweet disposition.

His mother's rights have been terminated and all his other brothers and sisters have been adopted. She never really had a chance with Jimmy, since she starved her second child to death. She said, "I didn't think he was hungry because he didn't say he was." She is not mean and cruel, but a rather sick woman. She loved him all she could.

I have lots of hope that Jimmy's mind will be stronger than his mom's. The other children are doing well and there is no sign of retardation. We had to take him to a neurologist and Early Childhood Intervention for evaluations before he was available for adoption.

The family that got this darling has a real treat. This boy is going somewhere in this world. He will make Martin Luther King, Michael Jordan, and Tiger Woods seem like distant memories. I wish you could be around him for at least a little while so you could fall in love with him too. I couldn't help but laugh at Mama Retta when, with her Alzheimer thinking said, "Little Jimmy is still as brown as the day he came here, he hasn't turned any whiter, yet." I guess she thought after living with all of us white people we would rub off onto him.

Our Jimmy was adopted by a single black lady. They took to each other immediately. She had never had children so this was a great need for both of these sweet people. This was another success story for us all.

BUD

We went to our local C.P.S. office to pick up our next little boy. Jose was four months old. I figured by his name I would be getting a little Spanish child. When I arrived to get our boy we all wondered who the mama was trying to convince that he was a Spanish baby. He was definitely a black child. We called him Bud. He was our second black child so we had a better idea of how to take care of him. Our first black baby, Jimmy, was given to us because of an overflow of children from Galveston, and they just didn't have enough foster homes for them all. We knew we wouldn't get to keep Bud in our home in Montgomery County for very long, because we have quite a few black foster families. It was just until C.P.S. could find an available home for him.

Bud was a sweet little one, and we enjoyed him very much. It wasn't long before they found a black foster home that needed him to add to their family. We dressed him up and styled his hair in an afro. He looked like Don King, the boxing promoter. The family that took him had the same last name as his, so that would save time and money if they decided to adopt him.

JOHN

Late one evening we got a call from C.P.S., wanting us to take a three month old boy. His mom and dad were using cocaine, and got into a big fight. The daddy was on probation, and had a bad habit of beating on the mama. Her track record didn't look real good either.

John was sweet, and needed lots of tender loving care. He was a solemn baby at first, and didn't seem to be happy. After he got used to us and the other kids, he opened up and smiled a lot. It wasn't long until he was laughing out loud. The mama's sister was trying to help her get her act together. It seemed to be working, and we were encouraged by her show of concern.

C.P.S. doesn't think like the average bear, and thought it was a good idea to put the baby back into the home. After all, it had been two weeks since the daddy had beat up the mama. And it was four weeks before that. Did they really think a wife beater was just going to stop beating her? I don't think so, although I'd sure like to see it happen to this very sweet, young couple. They are both so likeable. The mama was trying so hard, and the daddy was scared about breaking his probation.

We have high hopes that this family will always allow God to be first in their lives.

Good luck Johnnie.

ALENA

On a rainy Thursday, I made a trip to our local C.P.S. office to pick up Alena. She was a little nine month old girl. Her creepy mother had intentionally put her little foot in scalding water. She had a bad, bad, burn. The poor little darling must have been in such pain. We doctored the burn, and it gradually improved. Alena's four year old brother received a beating by the mother because he didn't watch the younger kids good enough.

As Alena's pain began to subside, she gradually cracked a smile. It wasn't long until she was feeling her oats. We enjoyed her, and tried to dress her and Jimmy in similar outfits. They were quite a team.

Alena's daddy is interested in getting custody of her. He has a track record of abusing his wife and kids. There will have to be a home study.

We have high hopes that the family will never be reunited unless there is a drastic change in their lives and lifestyles. Alena deserves to have a chance at a fantastic life.

COMMON SENSE AND CHILDHOOD HANDICAPS

Common sense should be used and human behavior should be taught to all employees of C.P.S. It would be very helpful if the people in authority would listen to the employees and foster parents, and if it is agreed that they are right, go with their decision. C.P.S. usually recommends what they wanted in the first place, then blame it on the judge for accepting their recommendations. C.P.S., in turn, washes their hands of the case, and the judge disowns any problems because he says it was what C.P.S. recommended. No one takes the responsibility and another child is put back into a tragic situation.

Some of our C.P.S. workers and judges are uniquely gifted for their jobs. They listen to their hearts while using their heads. Unfortunately, there are so few of them. So many of our judges, and many of our C.P.S. leaders, are afraid of sticking out their necks for any of our children, even when it's obvious to the lay person what needs to be done.

We know that C.P.S. and judges are under lots of pressure from birth parents, grandparents, and influential people that could take their jobs. But we need people in these positions that have enough morals and common sense to be willing to say they will be the one to make a difference.

I'm sure when they first started their work they planned on helping our children and changing the world for the better. But after many cases not panning out as expected, little by little the heart was taken over by pride. They soon became afraid of what people would do, or think, if they bucked the system.

There is never an ideal setting when placing the child back into the family. However, there is a big difference between unloading the child (from paperwork) and protecting the child. C.P.S. has a bad reputation of closing the case and eliminating all the paperwork, visits, and trouble. Again, out of sight, and out of mind.

No doubt there is an overload of paperwork, meetings, road work, visits, and court appearances. We foster parents can understand this and relate to it. But we still try to put the kids chances for a good life before the parents, grandparents, and all the others.

How many times have we heard from C.P.S. that, "The parents have done all we told them to so we have to give their child back." Even if they had beaten their babies six times daily and kept them in hot cars while they were drinking or making a drug deal, the kids were back in their custody if they had taken a parenting class and shown up for visitation every other week for an hour visit, with everyone's eyes on them.

Sometimes the parents have really proven that they will give it all they've got and try to be a good mama and daddy. And sometimes it is just ignorance and a cycle they are in. They really have not been taught how to be good parents, by example, or by anyone telling them, or showing them. Some are willing to learn and really want to give the kids a better life. These kind of parents need a chance to change. The ones with a track record of abuse and neglect time after time need their children placed into a loving, caring home that needs and wants a child.

The C.P.S. people I've dealt with are not cold, uncaring people. All the ladies and men I've been associated with are sweet, good, and loving people. Some have just forgotten where their priorities belong. They've forgotten their directions.

Nearly every foster parent has had cases where they fought for the child. Some have fought many battles, trying to do what's best for the kids, to no avail. Many have given up and stopped fostering. C.P.S. doesn't blink an eye, they just start with a new group of recruits that are fresh, nieve, and ready to put their trust in a losing cause. The foster parent who fights for the child is soon tagged as getting too involved with the child and having a hard time letting go. This takes away the guilt that C.P.S. should have accepted. Instead, they lay it on the foster parents, who know it's not smart to put them back into incest, beatings, neglect, etc.

So very many of our female C.P.S. workers aren't mama's so they cannot relate, or comprehend the full extend of the child's emotional needs. There are no amount of psychiatric books that take the place of a person's 24 hour a day experiences. One hour office calls don't equate with daily experiences. Most of the doctor's knowledge is coming from books other psychiatrists have written, and information gathered from the child's mom that works outside the home and gets home at 5:30 or 6:00 and has the child in bed by 8:00. It's hard for the doctor or mama to meet the full extent of the child's needs.

When we started fostering, we thought maybe our biggest problem would be a child telling us, "No" and, "Not going to," but it didn't take us long to find out these minor things were nothing.

We've worked with some wonderful home developers, caseworkers, and foster parents.

It was very hard giving up each child. A little piece of our heart would go with each of them. However, the ones that went back to incestuous or drug addicted and alcoholic homes would hurt the most. We fought all we could to protect them. When we did fight, we were accused of having a hard time giving them up. They would rather shift the blame to us, rather than accept the fact that the children needed help.

There are so many different disabilities that foster parents deal with. I'll discuss a few in the closing pages of this book.

FETAL ALCOHOL EFFECTED (F.A.E.)
FETAL ALCOHOL SYNDROME (F.A.S.)

The alcohol in the fetus causes irreversible brain damage and life with these children is filled with unwanted behaviors.

The child that has F.A.E. is the hardest to parent. He/she "looks" so normal and there are days that they have very normal and even good behavior. Then for some unknown reason everything falls apart, the F.A.E. does not have the facial abnormalities to "remind" you of his disabilities.

Fetal Alcohol Syndrome (F.A.S.) is a developmental disability caused by the effects of a mother drinking during pregnancy. F.A.S. is an organic brain disorder which manifests in central nervous system damage, growth deficiency and anti-social behaviors. It's a lifelong disability. The impact of F.A.S. on our society is great.

Many children with F.A.S. go undiagnosed. They are among those who are homeless, in prisons, and working the streets. Many are misdiagnosed, and are costing the state as much as $1,000 per day in psychiatric care, which is inappropriate. Some are serving prison terms for crimes done because of their inability to make judgments, or their lack of conscience. They are vulnerable to pressure to come in.

F.A.S. children are talkative, like to be the center of attention, impulsive, superficial, and manipulative. They have a hard time making, and keeping friends. They are unable to see another's perspective, and have problems understanding the consequences. They lie, steal, cheat, and are very often angry.

Their learning is very hampered by a lack of comprehension skills and shallow conversations. They may seem competent because of their chattiness. They have an attention deficit and a math difficulty, and are conartists. As the get older they have difficulty handling money, difficulty with decisions and judgments, and difficulty holding down a job.

F.A.S. is a hidden disability because it's seldom identified at birth. Early development may follow the normal curve, especially when retardation is borderline. The children do not have obvious handicaps. Their behaviors are initially seen as cute (chattiness, friendliness with strangers, love of attention). As they get into school age they may go undiagnosed, be misdiagnosed as emotionally impaired, or placed in classes for children with hyperactivity or behavioral disorders.

F.A.S. is not caused by poor parenting, neither is there enough love and patience to overcome the effects of F.A.S.. The children have great difficulty bonding.

A child with F.A.S. may often seem as though he follows logical thinking patterns and agrees with a plan of action. The next day he may have to reprocess the discussion, as though it were new information.

Children with F.A.S. are exhausting to the parents because of the 24 hour a day demands they make. They have difficulty with peers and siblings, school problems, untrustworthy behavior, hyperactivity, and sleep disturbances. Your life is taken up by this one child, so that your other children are robbed of your time.

Although exhausted, angry and often hopeless, parents often evidence bonding and love towards the child with F.A.S., and are able to separate the child from his behaviors, seeing him as a victim of pain.

Each child doesn't have every one of the symptoms. However, they have so many of the same symptoms, that it's hard to diagnose.

ATTACHMENT DISORDER

Sometimes we foster parents receive a child with an anti-social personality. This is the child that has an "Attachment Disorder." These children simply do not seem to view the world, or react to it, in ways that make sense to the rest of us. I believe the first three years are the most important years of a child's life. A tremendous amount of growth and development must take place in the human brain during these first few years. The brain begins by developing the areas that are most needed for survival. These areas are usually in the middle of the brain and are responsible for arousal, primitive memory storage, and control of movement.

In the right environment, babies are picked up and held, fed, and rocked when they cry, their diapers are changed, and someone talks to them and plays with them throughout the day. These activities are all needed for good brain development.

When babies are not picked up and held, are not provided with adequate sensory input, and are not moved frequently, the areas of their brains that are devoted to learning fail to develop as they should. Babies then do one of two things. They either begin to arouse and stimulate themselves by rocking, head banging, and other self-abusive behaviors, or they withdraw. Regardless of which of these options is chosen, the result is essentially the same. Huge areas of the brain fail to develop adequate skills for taking in information about the world around oneself, for processing and comprehending that information, and for planning some sort of appropriate response to it. Instead, children with Attachment

Disorder decide the world is an extremely hazardous place in which all kinds of dangerous, and often deadly events, can occur without warning, and that the best response is to be in control of everything they can control and to pretend to be in control of those things over which one has no control.

The symptoms are:
- Lack of ability to give and receive affection
- Superficially engaging and charming
- Self-destructive behavior
- Pathological lying
- Lying about the obvious (crazy lying)
- Stealing
- Cruelty to animals
- Lack of conscience
- Phoniness
- Lack of long-term childhood friends
- Abnormalities in eye control
- Learning disorders
- Indiscriminately affectionate with strangers
- Not affectionate with parents (not cuddly)
- No impulse controls
- Persistent nonsense, questions and incessant chatter
- Inappropriately demanding and clingy
- Lack of guilt or remorse
- Callous/lack of empathy
- Early behavioral problems
- Irresponsibility

Attachment is one of the most important concepts to understand, primarily because it affects our ability to form close relationships throughout our lives. The first three years of our lives sets the pattern we will go by the rest of our lives. The important elements of the child's gratification needs involves human touch, eye contact, emotion, and food.

Trust begins to develop along with social bonding. If the cycle is broken then trust will be stopped, or stifled, as will the social bonding process. This cycle appears to happen in the first three years of life. This early neglect or deprivation gives the child no ability to love, or feel guilt. There is no conscience, they have no idea of time, so they can't recall past experiences, and cannot benefit from past experiences or be motivated towards future goals. Psychologists state that deviant behavior suggests the individual is insensitive to other's opinions, he is characterized as a failure to respond to the ordinary motivation founded in respect or regard for others. This child is characterized by such things as excessive aggressiveness. These characteristics and symptoms attributed to the psychopathic youth are because of his lack of attachment. Lack of attachment allows the youthful psychopath to be free of all moral restraints, without guilt, without a conscience and without a superego.

It has been suggested that this type of child be educated early concerning his illness. This can potentially save them from jails, hospitals, rehabilitation programs, and institutions that the adults will require.

Most of our psychopathic parents were raised in abusive homes with dysfunctional parenting skills, devastated parents, single parents homes, impoverishment and/or were cared for in overly crowded day care centers.

We need a health care program that will offer community centers incentives for attendance and participation in such programs as:

1. Teaching parenting skills to help parents control themselves and their children.

2. Programs directed toward teaching parents how to love and nurture their children, and themselves, before the child is born, to help ease abuse.

3. Programs directed towards the community's youth by dealing with such issues as birth control, drug abuse prevention, and job training issues to slow the rate of unwanted births.

4. Educational programs that help to ease the poverty issues, although the youthful psychopathic offender is a problem which is found equally in all social economic societies, all races, all creeds, and national origins.

The criminal justice system is not prepared to deal with the youthful psychopathic offender within traditional means. We have tried so many things and failed, such as psychoanalysis. This didn't work because the unattached doesn't trust and is impulsive, cannot delay gratification and will not give up his control of others. Therapy doesn't work on the psychopath. They desperately need constant direction, due to their needs to manipulate.

Behavior modification has some effect on the psychopath, if he or she has a desire to change. Self motivators for the child include a continuously controlled system of rewards. A problem of behavior modification is that it requires constant control. Another problem in behavior modification programs is that within 18 months of the child's release, the child is no better off than before the treatments began.

Studies have shown that the psychopath's brain has lower levels of mood altering chemicals called Serolomin, than his peers. who are not psychopaths. These lower levels of Serolomin appear to be the link to why psychopaths seek out stimulation; some stimulation may even be painful to the individual. An example of this lower level of Serolomin is that psychopathic patients do not slow stress while being administered electric shocks. Psychopath's can distance themselves mentally from pain. Another example of the lower levels of Serolomin is that jailers have reported that electricity had to be increased in the electric chair to kill the psychopathic killers.

There are Attachment treatment programs that are recommended for children under the age of seven.

ATTENTION DEFICIT DISORDER

Sometimes we foster parents will receive a child suffering from Attention Deficit Disorder (A.D.D.). It is a problem frequently diagnosed that can be very frustrating and confusing to the family, the school, and the child. A.D.D. is a developmental disability which can occur with or without hyperactivity. Symptoms include problems with sustained attention, poor impulse control, and difficulty in regulation of their activity level. It is more common in boys than in girls, with a three to one ratio. It is widely accepted that A.D.D. is a neurological disorder where part of the brain is not working properly in terms of sustaining attention and controlling impulses. A.D.D. is not the result of poor parenting, and should not be treated as if it's an emotional problem.

It' s possible, that if not diagnosed and treated, it can result in an emotional problem. If a child has difficulty completing school assignments, he can develop poor self esteem. Approximately 35% of A.D.D. children also have learning disabilities. Most cases of A.D.D. are present at birth and it's believed to be is genetic. Many A.D.D. children have at least one parent who had the disorder.

Proper diagnosis involves a good assessment. The child's behavior should be assessed in a variety of settings, particularly at school. The possibility of learning disabilities should also be evaluated with psychological testing, especially if a child is doing poorly in school. The current treatment methods are designed to help the child and parents to cope with A.D.D., not cure it.

Early diagnosis and treatment can also prevent other problems from developing, such as depression and conduct problems. Long term studies following A.D.D. children into adulthood indicate that children frequently do not out grow this problem. Many adults are now treated for this disorder.

Treatment for A.D.D. children involves three areas:
1. Medication
2. Parental behavior management training
3. Structuring the child's school environment

Stimulant medication, such as Ritalin, helps the A.D.D. individual to sustain and focus his attention.

Behavior modification administered by parents and teachers helps the child by teaching him or her self-control. A.D.D. children often lack enough internal motivation to overcome this difficulty of staying focused on tasks, and need extra motivation and incentives. Various types of behavior modification programs are set up, depending on the age of the child. These programs should be used both at home and school. Structure in the classroom helps the A.D.D. child stay on task and organize his activities. Examples of classroom structure include minimizing distractions, posting rules and daily schedules, and giving one instruction at a time.

Once diagnosed primarily in school-age children, A.D.D. is now being diagnosed in a record number of adults. Several recent studies estimate that six to 9.5 million American adults have the disorder, making it as common as severe clinical depression or drug abuse.

Through a combination of medication and intensive counseling on ways to organize themselves and function in an office, many people who have the disorder build successful careers. For many others though, the remedies are too little and too late, and their careers suffer irreversible damage.

At the current pace, adults will receive 729,000 prescriptions or recommendations this year for Ritalin – a mild stimulant commonly used to treat the disorder – according to IMS America, Ltd., a pharmaceutical research company. In 1992, the number was just 217,000.

It has been said that having A.D.D. is not a curse. "It is like having a Ferrari engine under the hood. It can take you to plenty of interesting places, if you know how to manage it. Or it can take you into plenty of brick walls."

Concern is growing about the use of Ritalin as a recreational stimulant by college students and fast-track professionals.

The trend is already affecting America's corporate insurance claims. Ten years ago, virtually no employees who had group disability coverage from UNUM Corp, had ever filed a claim based on A.D.D. Last year, the disease showed up in less that half of one percent of the company's 53,000 cases.

This has not gone unnoticed by employers. Typically, large companies such as IBM consider the disorder a mental illness and cover it under an outpatient or hospitalization plan.

ATTENTION DEFICIT HYPERACTIVITY DISORDER

Attention Deficit Hyperactivity Disorder (A.D.H.D.) is even more hectic for the child and parent. With this kind of child the parent is tempted to take twice the amount of medication for himself than is prescribed for the child. They are so nerve racking, you stay on the edge of the cliff at all times. To be away from them for five minutes brings great pleasure for you. It's not that they are unlovable. It's just that they make it very hard to love them.

A.D.H.D. is the same as A.D.D. but with hyperactivity that never seems to stop. This child seems to fidget constantly, has difficulty remaining seated or playing quietly, and talks excessively.

CRACK BABIES

A very sad type of baby to get is the one that is addicted to cocaine, due to her mother's use of the drug during pregnancy.

It breaks my heart to see a baby having withdrawals and its little body shaking and drawing back. We have to wrap the child very tightly in a blanket for the only relief it can get.

PHYSICAL ABUSE

With physical abuse, you don't have to take the child to a psychiatrist to see that the child has two broken arms or burns all over its body.

SEXUAL ABUSE

Sexual abuse is not so easy to diagnose. Sometimes the child doesn't even know it's wrong that their folks, kin or neighbor has molested them. If a child is molested over a long period of time, he or she is sexually active and will try to molest other children, dolls, stuffed toys, etc. These kind of children need so very much counseling to try and make it through the rest of their life. People usually think twice before adopting the poor sexually abused child because they know how they act, as well as what has happened to their little bodies. Their bodies will heal faster than their way of thinking.

ADOPTION CRISIS

Texas is having quite an adoption crisis. Everyone wants a newborn blond, blue eyed, baby girl. Not many want the 10 year olds and older. There are match parties around the country to match foster kids with adoptive parents. It's very exciting as the children get their Sunday best clothes on, keep a smile on their face, and try to act as if this was their normal way of everyday life. They know how important the first impression is to sell themselves to these people. The prospective parents expect a little darling that always goes by the rules, obeys every time, and returns love and appreciation for a home they can give them. Never did they want to show their everyday temper or their anger over the fact that everyone prefers the little young children. Not many inquiries are made for these older children that could add so much to so many.

There are so very many people wanting to adopt a child. It's a shame that C.P.S. doesn't seem to realize that these children deserve a chance in life and so many of them should be permanently separated from their birth parents. C.P.S. feels the families should be reunited even if the parents have had chance after chance to take responsibility for their children. So often these babies are reunited with their birth parents, only to wind up back in the system again with other foster parents.

Foster parents beg, cry, fight, and do all they can do to protect the child. They point out How important it is to put the kids' protection before the parent or grandparent. I feel that all C.P.S. personnel should be required to be foster parents for at least one year, so they can have a better understanding from our angle.

PERSONAL SATISFACTION

Sometimes we foster parents envy people like judges, caseworkers, C.P.S. staff, and lawyers. What a blessing they have with their schedules, usually five days a week. After all, Foster parenting is a 24 hour, seven day a week, 365 day a year job. Others, when they wake up can choose to have a quiet breakfast, workout, then go to work, get a morning break for coffee or run to the Post Office or other short trips, back to work for a few hours, then it's lunch where you can eat by yourself or have adult friends to talk to that you don't have to wash their hands and face and get up every two minutes to keep the meal going. Back to work for a couple of hours, coffee break time. Now more free time to go shopping, golfing, plans with family, taking kids to baseball or show. Then maybe hours of uninterrupted TV with popcorn. Go to bed anytime you want to and sleep for six or eight hours straight.

Then Friday's here, watch out world, a weekend to call their own. They get all of the national holidays. If not feeling well, they can call in sick, and still get paid. Then there is vacation time. Maybe a trip to Colorado, or some other out of state location. We foster parents have to save up our pennies just to make to big trip to Cut-N-Shoot, which is a small community, only seven miles away, taking our children with us.

Even our bath time is not complete until a kid wants to come in to sit and watch. If we want to make a phone call to try to help our kids, we have to make it when it's nap time for them. Changing diapers, feeding the kids, and doctors visits can't wait. We have to work our protective phone calls in during their naps, which should be our relaxed, free time. Most times they don't take naps at the same time, so that eliminates whatever help we try to secure over the phone. So often, after we make those phone calls, the responsible people do not bother to return our calls. Many times they don't want to hear the problems we foster parents have, and they won't feel responsible when the child gets killed or hurt, if they know about it.

It's hard for us foster parents to carry on an adult conversation. Our big night out is our monthly C.P.S./Foster Parent meeting which just one of us can attend, while the other babysits. The meetings are designed to discuss children for two hours. Twenty four hours a day is not enough, and we are required so many meetings a year.

All foster parents have fears of allegations of abuse in our homes. It seems that the allegations are more frequent with the older children. So many of our people's lives have been ruined by some known habitual liar that gets mad, and is ready to move on to something else or doesn't want to go by their house rules, which we all have. The children know how the system works, and know how to punch the right button for attention, knowing they will be taken out of the home immediately. I'm not saying abuse doesn't occur sometimes in our foster homes. When our people are accused, they are so embarrassed, scared, and humiliated, that they don't fight back because they don't want to draw attention to their case. Their names are put on the police file and stays there until they can prove the incident did not happen. The child doesn't have to have any proof, but the accused individual has to prove their innocence. Their is no greater hurt in foster care than the fear that this will stay with you the rest of your life, when you, your family, and friends know nothing ugly happened.

It has been said to all of us that we need to know how to survive, when we are accused not, if we are accused. We have been blessed and not been accused, but so many of our friends have gone through this horrible procedure. Our hearts break for them because so many have given so much to the children they've helped, and the beauty of their great deeds have been marred for life by false accusations. It's overwhelming. They believe they've been given a wonderful blessing of caring for so many children, only to swallow the bitter pill of accusations cropping back into their precious memories.

We always hear that "Silence is golden," but sometimes when you miss out on the opportunity to defend or protect the innocent, then silence is the door of consent. You may be the next one to find yourself in a similar predicament, with no support from the system.

With all the advantages that these other professions and regular jobs offer, there is not one that can give me the fulfillment that being a foster parent can. At my age (past 25), I've done quite a few things that I've enjoyed, but God has never given me a job that's been more satisfying and rewarding. I don't miss the traveling, expensive clothes, furniture, houses and all the good things that we have come to expect as we grow older. These 36 babies we've had have more than fulfilled those wants and needs.

We had three sets of brothers, five sets of brothers and sisters, and 19 children without siblings. We were surprised that we never had any sets of sister.

The boys outnumbered the girls three to one. With all the foster children in homes all over America, it makes me proud of all the children getting help, but it always scares me, thinking of the thousands that are in such pain, and will never be helped. There is no better calling or job in the world than being foster parents.

So many people think if you are not working out in the public, you must have plenty of time on your hands. But we homemakers feel that not only do the employed have more time, they are also getting paid for their work.

God chose us for this job and there is not a college degree, job position, cash, power, or any other thing else that can meet the satisfaction, fulfillment, and blessings of helping to mold little people for our world. It has been said, "Babies being born is a sign that God wants the world to go on." And on it will go, until the end of time, as we know it.

Copies of this book can be obtained from:

B. J. Davis
111 Park Manor
Conroe, Texas 77301